The Whole Matter

Thomas Kinsella, 1992.

The Whole Matter

The Poetic Evolution of Thomas Kinsella

Thomas H. Jackson

The Lilliput Press, Dublin

Copyright © 1995 by Syracuse University Press
Syracuse, New York 13244-5160

All Rights Reserved

First Edition 1995
95 96 97 98 99 00   6 5 4 3 2 1

Illustrations courtesy of the author.

Permission by Thomas Kinsella to reprint lines from his poetry is gratefully acknowledged.

Permission to reprint lines from the poem "Spring Strains" of William Carlos Williams is also acknowledged. Copyright © 1938 by New Directions Publishing Corporation. Copyright © 1982, 1986 by William Eric Williams and Paul H. Williams. Reprinted by permission of New Directions Publishing Corporation.

A CIP record for this book is available from the British Library.
ISBN 1 874675 68 6 (cloth) 1 874675 57 0 (paper)

Acknowledgments
The Lilliput Press received financial assistance from
An Chomairle Ealafon / The Arts Council, Ireland

Manufactured in the United States of America

To the memory of Harry and Annie Jackson

Thomas H. Jackson is professor of English at Bryn Mawr College. He is the author of *The Early Poetry of Ezra Pound* and articles on modernist poetics, translation, and African fiction. Currently at work on a study of the poetry of D. H. Lawrence, he is also principal trombonist with the Main Line Symphony Orchestra in Pennsylvania.

Contents

Illustrations

Preface

Implicit in this book is the conviction that Thomas Kinsella is the most important and the most compendious Irish poet since Yeats. With respect to Ireland itself, his work in its totality performs a cultural task of central importance, however the ultimate reputations of Kinsella and his major contemporaries finally get sorted out. The work of reclamation he has done furnishes, I suggest, an exemplary base on which other poets can build, whether they particularly like his poetry or not. This is something that even Yeats did not fully perform. Yeats went to the Gaelic past and, to an extent beyond the reach of his Revivalist confreres, made it poetically useful and often respectable. He demonstrated that such material, whether the stuff of Gaelic myth and legend or the fanciful lore of faeries, could be woven into major poems. Kinsella does something else: he knits that material to a sensibility, a consciousness, showing not how to make an Irish past something to write about, but how to make it truly part of yourself—your creative self, if you happen to be a poet. But he also weaves it, as indeed he weaves that creative self, into the life around him, into its history and into the day-to-day reality of its events. Everything his speaker looks upon he looks upon with a mind informed by every aspect of Irish history and prehistory, never losing hold on rationality in the grip of emotion or on emotion, in a deep sense, in the grip of rational judgment.

And his pertinence is by no means limited to an Irish experience. He brings to every poem a multilevel awareness unique, so far as I know, in contemporary letters. One of the major convictions of his poetry is that a seamless continuity links persons, events, books, political events, and levels of the individual self. The term I use in discussing this aspect of his work since *Nightwalker* is *isomorphism;* personal experiences repeatedly turn out to be isomorphic with social or historical events, one mode of experience with another. Personal history can be isomorphic with family history, and both can be isomorphic with the history of a nation or nations. The term is not an exhaustive description of Kinsella's work, but it is undeniable that the ideal (and reality) of wholeness lies at the core of his poetry. The effects can be seen in the very shaping of his poetic practices. Turning from stylistic, and stylish, influences like Auden, turning even from his occasional echoing of his honored compatriot Austin Clarke, he finds in Joyce, in Jung, in Pound and Williams the motivation to a more inclusive form of attention. (Even the practice of translation comes gradually to seem to him an aspect of positive inclusion, of recuperation. Quite apart from the content of, say, *The Táin* or the lyrics in the anthology *An Duanaire,* the activity of translation in Kinsella's career can be taken to present an almost prototypical instance of the interaction of self and other that is constituted by almost any "original" poem.)

The process of achieving the ability to manifest this totalizing vision of reality is the principal focus of the chapters that follow. That process involved one of the most remarkable moves in the history of poetry in this century: Kinsella launched on a fifteen-year pursuit of the depth he came to realize his art demanded. He had to transcend—in fact, abandon—the dazzling yet conventional mastery that made his early work so remarkable and so successful, turning his back on creative practices and a style that had already made him one of the most esteemed poets in Ireland. (I use the term *conventional* not pejoratively, but certainly as implying limits and limitations.) In this book I have tried to trace out the stages and the concomitants of that astonishing project.

After an account in the first chapter of his early work (admittedly from the standpoint of later developments), I try to follow his course as he comes to build on—"incorporate" might be the conventional word, but not the accurate one—his insights into Jung, the lessons of Joyce, and the liberating examples of the American modernists, as he works to free himself from the limitations of conventional lyric form and attitudes. I mean quite seriously what I say at the end of chapter 5: that Kinsella emerges from this developmental process not as a strong simple self but as a consciousness more or less continuous with what it speaks of. What I mean is connected with my reluctance to use the word "incorporation," or its stylish cousin, "appropriation," with reference to Kinsella and his precursors. For as a poet, he is an example of Walter Benjamin's ideal translator, the figure characterized in "The Task of the Translator" not as giving a new individualized "rendition" of the original text, but as constituting its afterlife—as being, in other words, one of its offspring. Kinsella in a way *becomes,* or becomes an extending of, what an earlier terminology would call his influences. He takes up the life that is in Joyce, or Jung, or Pound, or early Irish poetry. He is what he is in part because of what he made of them, but what he made of them is a function of what he himself is. Again, what is at issue, I think, is that question of wholeness or continuity. Kinsella's transactions with Joyce or Jung are indeed just that, *trans*actions, as are his confrontations with Irish myths and poems, and the confrontations with the events and experiences that figure in his poetry.

Though this is the first book-length study of the work of Thomas Kinsella, the path to such an undertaking has been marked for some time by the work of several able practitioners. The Jungian aspect of Kinsella's work is visible in the poetry itself and certainly not unknown to readers who have followed his career; but it was voluminously and very helpfully documented in Carolyn Rosenberg's monumental doctoral dissertation, "Let Our Gaze Blaze: The Recent Poetry of Thomas Kinsella" (1980). Nor is the purview of that huge volume limited to the presence of Jung; it is a mine of information and critical acumen about matters biographical, numerological, literary, and mystical. The Jungian aspect was later explicated, with greater critical acuity, in Dillon Johnston's *Irish Poetry after Joyce* (1985). Robert Garratt's *Modern Irish Poetry: Tradition and Continuity from Yeats to Heaney* (1986) included a chapter on Kinsella, necessarily general, but a helpful move toward contextualizing Kinsella for an American audience.

Kinsella's Irish critics have been particularly acute. An issue of *Tracks* (no. 7, 1987) devoted exclusively to Kinsella included one of the best essays on his work, W. J. McCormack's "Politics or Community: Crux of Thomas Kinsella's Aesthetic Development," but the number as a whole is well worth reading. The mid-eighties were a gala time for Kinsella criticism, for in addition to the writings already cited, Seamus Deane in 1985 brought out *Irish Revivals: Essays in Modern Irish Literature 1880–1980*, which included what is probably the most insightful short essay on Kinsella to date. I was pleased to find there a degree of coincidental support for my own characterization of Kinsella's work as "compendious."

Kinsella's work, then, has not been without able critics, but this book carries out the first large-scale critical scrutiny of his work as a whole. Though I began by saying that he is the most important Irish poet since Yeats, it has been my hope that my discussion of his work will show him to be one of the major poets of our time, regardless of nationality. Since his earliest work he has become difficult—but he is also, as Ezra Pound says about all good poetry, *bracing*. At a time when the powers of human

mind and feeling seem debased on the one hand and thwarted and crip-
pled on the other by seemingly implacable and certainly corrupt forces the
world over, he presents us with rich and powerful experiences of mind
and feeling that demonstrate the life-sustaining power of human
consciousness.

A significant part of the research for this book was made possible by a
generous series of small grants from Bryn Mawr College, and a great
portion of the writing was accomplished during a sabbatical leave.
Thomas and Eleanor Kinsella were very generous with their time and
candor over a period of years, as was William J. McCormack, who was
also a vitally stimulating motivator of thought. Sean White was an indispensable contributor of information about the Dublin of Kinsella's—and
his—youth, and his gratuitous sacrifice of time to my needs was not the
least of my remarkable experiences in Dublin. The help I received from
Eamon Grennan and Aidan Clarke was very important to my understanding of the Irish setting. Vincent Sherry of Villanova University planted
the seed for the book by asking me to write the article on Kinsella for the
Dictionary of Literary Biography, and he was further helpful with bibliogra-
phy and general cheering on. Sheldon Brivic of Temple University aided
my dealings with *Finnegans Wake.* Though my greatest debt is to the
Kinsellas, Dillon Johnston was immensely generous with advice and assistance. Much of what I came to know in the way of Kinsella scholarship
were things I was steered to by him, and the comments he made as reader
of the manuscript for the Syracuse University Press have made this a better
book than it would have been without him.

Abbreviations

References to collections of Thomas Kinsella's poems are abbreviated and cited parenthetically, as follows:

AS	*Another September*
BF	*Blood and Family*
D	*Downstream*
HVS	*Her Vertical Smile*
N	*Nightwalker and Other Poems*
NLD	*Notes from the Land of the Dead*
P	*Poems 1956–1973*
PcP	*Peppercanister Poems 1972–1978*
PP	*Personal Places* (Peppercanister 14)
SP	*Songs of the Psyche*

The Whole Matter

Introduction

If a career like Ezra Pound's or, say, Hart Crane's is still exemplary at this late date, the typical early difficulty for anyone setting up as poet in the United States would seem to be the need to reinvent the wheel. In the absence of any strong tradition of poetry, of anything like a national sense of what poetry should or might be like, and of any strong national respect for either the art or its practitioners, the neophyte American poet typically has had to define the art anew—even to invent himself or herself as an artist. In more convention-bound cultures like England or Ireland, with more uniform national education, the corresponding hindrance is apt to be a prevailing sentiment that the wheel and the art had been quite well taken care of some time ago, thank you, long before *you* put yourself forward.[1] The culture into which Thomas Kinsella gradually inserted himself as a new poet in the 1950s was a far more literary one than what an American poet would encounter.[2] But the danger in a country that focuses a national education policy and the concomitant educational practices on a too firmly defined sense of its cultural tradition is that the culture may

1. Thus Hélène Cixous in "The Laugh of the Medusa" (writing of France, to be sure, and women, but the atmosphere is not unique to France): "And why don't you write? . . . Because writing is at once too high, too great for you, it's reserved for the great—that is, for 'great men' " (Cixous 1981, 246).
2. Cf. Lyons 1973, 651: "The most striking conclusion to be drawn from a study of the papers actually taken by the students at the Leaving Certificate—the more important of the two examinations from the career point of view—is that secondary education in Ireland retains to the present day a strong literary bias." The Civil Service Kinsella entered (when he joined the Department of Finance) was still, moreover, an elite service; it had its pick of the top hundred or so school leavers every year, and it is still said to be peppered with writers and would-be writers. Kinsella's early books were reviewed—and not merely as colleagueal curiosities—in the *Civil Service Review*.

1

be a dead one and populated, moreover, not so much by ossified figures of the past as by ossified illusions. Thus Hugh Kenner can quote from Patrick Kavanagh's short-lived paper the drearily Philistine comments of Mr. T. O'Deirg, Minister for Lands, in 1952, to the effect that "it was a pity that there was not now the close connection between the poets and the people such as existed fifty years ago." Mr. O'Deirg hoped to see a revival "of popular poetry that would bring nationality to its bosom such as Ethna Carberry did in her time."[3] Ethna Carberry was the pen name of Anna Johnston (born 1866, obit. 1902), cofounder of the Gaelic-culture magazine *Shan Van Vocht* and author of a poem about the voyage of the *Erin's Hope* ("A sail, wind-filled from out the West! our waiting time is done; / Since sword and spear and shield are here to free our hapless One!"). It is not clear why Mr. O'Deirg's shaky grammar cited her rather than some better-known colleague—perhaps W. B. Yeats.

Every age—every month—of course has its fatuous politicians, but commenting historians as well as eyewitnesses of the time seem unanimously agreed on the dreariness of the Irish fifties. Ireland was still in the grips of the cultural and economic doldrums that had beset the country since Independence, still grieving over the wound that had torn away its industrial northeast and continuing, it would seem, to confuse parochialism and provinciality with national integrity. With respect to literary life, there were a handful of short-lived little magazines—John Ryan's *Envoy,* David Marcus's *Irish Writing,* Kavanagh's *Weekly,* and the *Kilkenny Magazine,* but until the founding of Liam Miller's Dolmen Press there was no publisher in Ireland for books of poetry by Irish writers,[4] and even Miller's enterprise, in which Kinsella played an important role, was for a long time something of a kitchen-table operation. Moreover, if the handful of little magazines in the late forties and early fifties give the impression of a lively up-and-coming generation of new poets, inspection of the tables of contents tends to yield the same names over and over: Clarke, Kavanagh, Valentin Iremonger, Anthony Cronin, James Liddy, Pearse Hutchinson, and, eventually, Thomas Kinsella: not quite a horde, even for so small a nation as Ireland. There were, or had been, two possibly major figures; but one, Austin Clarke, was wasting his time on reviewing (like Pound years before), and the other, Patrick Kavanagh, was seething in the relatively sterile rage of the contemned and patronized alien clown.

On the other hand, if you are one of a half-dozen young poets barely

---

3. Cited in Kenner 1983, 242. *Kavanagh's Weekly,* of course, was the publication of the redoubtable Patrick Kavanagh—for as long as his funding lasted.
4. See Skelton 1965.

or not yet out of college, sitting around a table plotting aesthetic revolution, things can look fairly lively if you don't step out into the street. Alan Simpson stepped into the street, so to speak, in 1957, when he mounted a production of Tennessee Williams's *Rose Tattoo*. He found himself the target of a police prosecution for presenting an indecent performance that took him a full year to resolve; the year after, the archbishop of Dublin, with the support of the Dublin Trade Unions, managed to put the kibosh on a Dublin theater festival that wanted to stage a dramatization called *Bloomsday* along with some mimes by Beckett. Censorship of this sort seems to have represented the fag end of an Irish Ireland movement that was mounted after Independence and which blended all too well with the Church's fastidiousness about "moral" (sc., "sexual") matters under the umbrella of official censorship.[5] Writing of Clarke's career in 1974, Kinsella himself began with the remark that "In those flat years in Ireland at the beginning of the nineteen fifties, depressed so thoroughly that one scarcely noticed it, the uneasy silence of Austin Clarke added a certain emphasis" (Kinsella 1974, 128).

Not quite a decade earlier he had spoken of his own situation as a poet in Ireland out of an isolation it is to be hoped few poets ever have to confront. Looking at Irish poets writing in either Irish or English, he said, "the word 'colleagues' fades on the lips before the reality: a scattering of incoherent lives. . . . I can learn nothing from them except that I am isolated" (Kinsella 1970, 51). This is a remark about loneliness, perhaps, and concerns the life of the poet, but he goes on to address issues far more deep-running. The principal issue the poet addresses in "The Irish Writer" is the difficulty any Irish poet experiences in finding, and feeling, an identity, a difficulty arising from the terrible *ungroundedness* Kinsella feels at this point to be the plight of anyone who would be a poet in Ireland. The country, of course, has a rich literary past, but of those riches Kinsella said, "I recognize simultaneously a great inheritance and a great loss. The inheritance is mine, but only at two enormous removes—across a century's silence and through an exchange of worlds" necessitated by the "calamity" that was the death of the Irish language. He quotes sympathetically the complaint of Daniel Corkery: "Everywhere in the mentality of the Irish people are flux and uncertainty. Our national consciousness may be described, in a native phrase, as a quaking sod. It gives no footing. It is not English, nor Irish, nor Anglo-Irish" (Kinsella 1970, 60). With the present profitless and the past locked away, Kinsella concludes that "The only semblance of escape—consonant with integrity—is into a greater

---

5. See Brown 1985, chaps. 1, 2, and 7; and Lyons 1973, 685–93.

isolation." At this stage in Thomas Kinsella's work it seems that wherever the poet turns he confronts isolation and irrelevance. How far-reaching such feelings were in Kinsella's earliest writing can be seen in one of the impressively ambitious poems in his first major collection, "Baggot Street Deserta." It is a meditation on poetry at once ambitious and grim, calling the ethical standing of the art into question even as it asserts the continuity of poetry with nature itself and with human endeavor in general. Early in the poem a semianimate nature engages with the speaker's pathetic fallacies:

> The window is wide
> On a crawling arch of stars, and the night
> Reacts faintly to the mathematic
> Passion of a cello suite
> Plotting the quiet of my attic.
> A mile away the river toils
> Its buttressed fathoms out to sea;
> Tucked in the mountains, many miles
> Away from its roaring outcome, a shy
> Gasp of waters in the gorse
> Is sonnetting origins.
>
> (*AS*, 29)

His sleeping fellow citizens unconsciously perform their version of his creative activities, as "Dreamers' heads / Lie mesmerised in Dublin's beds / Flashing with images, Adam's morse."

But the fruits of this unwitting unity are not much: to the "lingering threadbare cry" of a curlew the poet adds his

> call of exile, half-
> Buried longing, half-serious
> Anger and the rueful laugh.
> We fly into our risk, the spurious.

And the reason for this is gloomily sweeping:

> Versing, like an exile, makes
> A virtuoso of the heart,
> Interpreting the old mistakes
> And discords in a work of Art
> For the One, a private masterpiece
> Of doctored recollections. Truth

Concedes, before the dew, its place
In the spray of dried forgettings Youth
Collected when they were a single
Furious undissected bloom.

The modernist dream of poetry as cognition receives this grim dismissal:

Out where imagination arches
Chilly points of light transact
The business of the border-marches
Of the Real, and I—a fact
That may be countered or may not—
Find their privacy complete.

It is characteristic of the early Kinsella that such verbal virtuosity should be deployed to assert its own futility—the poet-speaker clearly will entertain no illusions about any putative continuity of mind with reality. One finds in the early Kinsella a poet of great verbal skill manifesting again and again a conviction of the limited power of his own impressive art and a sense of his own randomness, shut out from the real by the very nature of reality and cut off from any nurturing past by the depredations of history. For some years during the early stages of his career, the most he would claim for his art in general was that "one of the main impulses to poetry . . . is an attempt more or less to stem the passing of time; it's the process of arresting the erosion of feelings and relationships and objects which is being fought by the artist. . . . he is there to combat the erosion" (Orr 1966, 106). Such talk constitutes a considerable retreat, if the term is fair, from the major traditions of English-language poetry—certainly from the claims of the major Romantic poets and the major modernists—a retreat, perhaps, toward the attitudes of the Movement poets across the Irish Sea.[6]

And yet the modern Ireland that produced Thomas Kinsella stems from a culture that ascribed great powers and great importance to poetry, and the art itself in Ireland can claim weighty historical sanctions. The practice Wordsworth may have been emulating in grouping some of his works as "Poems on the Naming of Places," for example, goes far, far back in Irish poetry. Not all the *dindshenchas,* the lore of high places and of

6. By whom, however, he does not seem to have been very impressed. See his review of *New Lines* in the *Irish Press* (1 Dec. 1956), where he describes the writers in that anthology as "the school of University poets" who present "a common front of intellectualized unecstatic verse." Those comments are not thrown out scornfully, but they make Kinsella's feelings about that kind of poetry pretty clear.

place names, were written in verse, but a large proportion were. Compiling such lore was an important function of poets in ancient Ireland, and it is not far-fetched to connect this fact with the striking prominence of nature poetry in the Irish past. The great scholar Kuno Meyer wrote that "To seek out and love Nature, in its tiniest phenomena as in its grandest, was given to no people so early and so fully as [to] the Celt." Commenting on this characteristic of Celtic literature, Seamus Heaney remarks on the "love of place and lamentation against exile from a cherished territory" which is a "typical strain in the Celtic sensibility" (Heaney 1980, 182, 184). Modern poems like MacNiece's "River in Spate" make it clear that this strain has by no means died out—and his "Train to Dublin" simply focuses it on an object that happens to be European industrial rather than Bronze Age Celtic. More and more Kinsella's own work comes to be liberally marked by the echo, if not certainly the effects, of this tradition —like the late poems "38 Phoenix Street" and "Bow Lane," the relatively early "Phoenix Park" expands a place into its meaning, and the poet's use of the drawing of Dublin's Peppercanister church as the emblem for all his Peppercanister series speaks for itself as an appeal to place and the significance of its name.

Nor was explaining place names the only official and quasi-official function of poets. As in other heroic cultures, Gaelic poets were the recorders of great deeds and great events. The *Senchus Mor*, a compilation of ancient Irish law, states that "until the coming of Patrick speech was not suffered in Ireland but to three: to a historian for narrative and the relating of tales; to a poet for eulogy and satire; to a brehon lawyer for giving judgment according to the old tradition and precedent" (Flower 1947, 4). Robin Flower, from whose book that passage is taken, points out that "the name *fili*, 'poet,' originally with a wider meaning 'seer,' comprehended all these functions of the men of learning in pre-Christian Ireland" (4).

Flower's reference to the meaning *seer* reflects the fact that in some old texts the terms *fili* and *drui*, druid or prophet, or seer, were interchangeable (Knott and Murphy 1966, 21). According to the *Lebor Gabála Erenn*, the Book of the Takings of Ireland, when the sons of Mil, the true stock of the Irish people as we know them, arrived on the shores of Ireland, the first act was the improvisation of a poem-prayer by Amargin, who in himself combined the roles of leader, warrior, and poet (Macalister 1956).

The *fili* was not a wandering minstrel nor yet an undergraduate taking creative writing as an elective. In times less legendary than the days of Amergin, the *fili* was a member of a true literary elite who earned his place through an astonishingly arduous professional training. In the first place, it was a strictly hereditary calling. And it seems there were no less than seven grades of poet; the highest required the mastering of seven years of training—fourteen years, according to one source. We can get some idea of the fantastic labor involved from the fact the tenth-century *Book of Armagh* lists 350 distinct meters—of which practicing bards tended to make use of 100 (Power 1967, 32). Add the information that the training was entirely oral and that bardic poems often ran to the neighborhood of a hundred quatrains, and it is plain that the status of the *fili* was no soft touch. The usual method of training seems to have involved the assignment of a topic to the trainee, who would lie solitary in a dark room composing his poem in his head. When it was ready, according to Power, "light and paper were brought in and the young man wrote down his efforts." It remains to add only that the metrical intricacy of these compositions staggers the modern imagination; they make something like *Comus* seem the merest *bijou*.[7]

What made this fantastic labor worthwhile was the public standing enjoyed by this privileged class of artists. They were indispensable appurtenances of any court, wielders of a skill of positively divine importance, and by the late Middle Ages, graduate *filid* could go job hunting with all the confidence with which holders of Ivy League law degrees would for a time pursue jobs on Wall Street. Satire was a potentially mortal weapon at the disposal of poets, and much feared. "Greedie of praise they be," wrote Robert Stanihurst of Irish kings, "and fearfull of dishonour, and to this end they esteeme their poets who write Irish learnedlie and pen their sonets heroicall, for the which they are bountifullie rewarded, if not they send out libels in dispraise, thereof the lords and gentlemen stand in great awe" (Knott and Murphy 1966, 77–78). Caiér, king of Connacht, lost his throne when his nephew, the poet Néde, subjected him to a satire so scathing that it raised blisters on his face; a king with a blemish is unfit to rule, and Caiér fled in shame. Joyce was pursuing this tradition in conducting his vendetta against Oliver St. John Gogarty in the pages of *Ulysses,* and that self-congratulatory poetaster subscribed to it himself in his anxiety over the knowledge that Joyce was prepared to satirize him in the figure of Buck Mulligan.

7. Consider, for example, Hyde's account of the combining of *aird-rinn* and *deibhidh* meter: the rhyming word which ends the second line of a pair must "contain a syllable more than the rhyming word which ends the first, while if the accent fall in the first line on the ultimate syllable it mostly falls in the second line on the penultimate, if it falls on the penultimate in the first line it generally falls on the antepenultimate in the second" (Hyde 1906, 483–84).

On the one hand, then, there was that dormant precedent, and a vast body of vigorous and honorable cultural history for poets to tap if they could, though they would have to tap it with more vitality and authenticity than had characterized the gestures of the Revivalists and their successors. On the other hand, we have Kinsella and other Irish writers in the middle of this century claiming one way or another to be operating in a poetic wasteland. Thomas Kinsella's recovery of the energizing power of that tradition is one of the most impressive developments in contemporary letters.

He certainly begins at what seems the furthest possible remove from the history whose outlines I have just traced. His conception of the artistic act was the source of stringent limits he set to both language and imagination, which produced, in his first major collection, *Another September,* a poetry like that in "Baggot Street Deserta," scrupulously *bounded.* The young Kinsella is perfectly serious about his art, but he is most reluctant to make any grandiose claims for it. For the early Kinsella, poetry is at best a holding force resisting the inevitable processes of entropy.

A reader taking up Kinsella's early collections—*Poems, Another September,* even *Downstream*—might be puzzled by those remarks about stemming the passage of time and arresting erosion, and might well feel that the poems do not so much stem the passage of time and the process of erosion as lament their inevitability, or at any rate that they leave quite open the question of just how the stemming is to be seen as taking place. Not that "feelings and relationships and objects" must mean only concrete physical facts. A clear or striking conception, for example—which might stem only from an effectual collocation of words—may be triumphantly preserved by the order of the poem, as in the closing section of "The Fifth Season":

> Some, who have comely daughters, watch
> A spray of God's wit light the gloom,
> A tree of nerves vividly breaking.
> All that drifts into the tomb
> Is a body still or a body speaking.
>
> (*AS,* 35)

Lines like those, with their complicated vowel patterns approaching assonance—*comely* against *gloom, speaking* against *breaking,* the vowels of *vividly* against those of *light, body* against *tomb,* and so on—probably reflect Kinsella's qualified admiration of Austin Clarke, but in any case they seem to aim at an experience intricate but, like the effects of his temporary enthusiasm for Auden, chiefly verbal. A manifestation of limit in dealing with a scene more vividly external occurs in the early poem "Lead." There the speaker meditates on two ancient leaden dice he has found at Luttrell's Glen and toward the end of the poem contemplates the implications of their making:

> Drowned in a leafy dusk, paused over metal,
> The mind leaped towards the clash of the real.
> Its leather-vizored workmen, stuped in flame
> And stumbling about such forges, in their time
> Roofed many a teeming manor
> With sheeted calms no violence could dispel;
> Now stood as the light encircled them
> Blinded against their black-and-ruddy banner;
>
> Then plunged into the columned Autumn burning.
> Craft and craftsman, risen out of nothing,
> Sank to a jackdaw chatter in the head.
> The road to Dublin churned back into mud.
> Gaea, naked as slate,
> Caught in her fern those quenched eyes, scarred with seeing
> Let drop like dice the aproned dead
> Stretched in silence under this estate.
>
> (*AS*, 45)

The vigor of mind here is unmistakable; the speaker has clearly formulated for himself a vivid sense of process and personal meaning. He has articulated a strong experience and thereby preserved it from loss, as well as gaining an experience in the process of articulation itself. On the other hand, the speaker's mind does run to the fact that these ancient lead workers must have made roofs, their most significant work something that bespoke the necessary separateness of self and other, and the speaker's closing thought is of the "aproned dead," utterly finite, "Let drop like dice / Stretched in silence under this estate." The precise articulation of an experience—any experience—then, is a means of stemming loss, but that is as much as honesty will allow the early Kinsella to claim. Turning aside as mere indulgence the imputation to poetry of any meaningful consolatory power, this work is almost uncompromisingly stoical. At the time of the 1966 interview with Peter Orr, Kinsella was concerned to say that the poet must rise above partisan involvement in the subject matter of his verse and that "the quality of the instant itself . . . doesn't impose any actual, necessary, stateable conditions" on the poem. There is an anxiety here about the autonomy of the poem that Kinsella would eventually cease to worry about, a desire to protect the poem, as a matter of aesthetic purity, from the encroachments of the nonliterary. He recognized some such considerations in a later interview, where he remarked that "I think at the beginning my poems were influenced by literature more than by fact. I would regard the direct dealing with matter as something that requires great sophistication and equipment." "For the moment," he went on to say, "it would appear to me that the artistic act has to do with the eliciting of order from significant experience, so as to come to terms with that experience on the basis of understanding of some kind" (Haffenden 1981, 104). There is a slight but significant difference between these two sets of remarks, and the straightforwardness with which we can take the earlier statements is attested to by the very form of the early work. "Mirror in February," the last poem in *Downstream,* already involves a move away from the staid stoicism of his very earliest work, but for all its skill, its language seems cautious and limited in the light of the work that would come later:

> Below my window the awakening trees,
> Hacked clean for better bearing, stand defaced
> Suffering their brute necessities,
> And how should the flesh not quail that span for span
> Is mutilated more? In slow distaste
> I fold my towel with what grace I can,
> Not young and not renewable, but man.
>
> (*D,* 63)

Stoic or not, this is highly expressive, and the imagery is perfectly adequate to its purpose—but it is certainly not unconventional. The structure of the mournful wit in *bearing* and *defaced* is not beyond the powers of rational perception; the speaker has found some fortuitous verbal relations —an order—in a world given over to otherwise shapeless entropy. Indeed, the strategy of the whole poem is the fairly straightforward one of simply naming things or situations and then meditating on them:

> The day dawns with scent of must and rain,
> Of opened soil, dark trees, dry bedroom air.
> Under the fading lamp, half-dressed—my brain
> Idling on some compulsive fantasy—
> I towel my shaven lip and stop, and stare,
> Riveted by a dark exhausted eye,
> A dry downturning mouth.

It seems again that it is time to learn,
In this untiring, crumbling place of growth
To which, for the time being, I return.
Now plainly in the mirror of my soul
I read that I have looked my last on youth
And little more; for they are not made whole
That reach the age of Christ.

(*D*, 63)

This deliberate boundedness has significant concomitants. To compare Kinsella's early poems with work by his contemporaries, poets like John Montague and Richard Murphy, or even a later contemporary such as Seamus Heaney, is to be struck by the latter poets' ties to landscape and place, to history and to Ireland, which Kinsella—the early Kinsella, at any rate—only sometimes shares. For good historical reasons those poets seem almost burdensomely conscious of their Irishness early in their careers, insistently localist in their subjects and their themes. It is tempting to see Kinsella's avoidance of such orientations and his early assertion that his poetry was "completely separate" from his status as either an Irishman or a quondam Catholic (Orr 1966, 107) almost as a kind of self-exile—a strategy functioning, like his pursuit of the intricacies of assonantial verse, to afford him some untroubled space within which to carve a secure aesthetic arena.[8]

A mere half-dozen years after *Another September,* however, in *Notes from the Land of the Dead* the mode of discourse and the conceptual orientation have undergone a radical change. In "A Hand of Solo" the speaker as a boy bites into a pomegranate: "I sank my teeth in it," he says,

loosening the packed mass of dryish beads
from their indigo darkness.
I drove my tongue among them

and took a mouthful, and slowly
bolted them.

(*NLD*, 15)

The action imaged here is the temporal precursor of the action with which the poem begins:

8. Donald Davie noticed this aspect of Kinsella's work as early as 1957. He found in *Poems* of 1956 a kind of poem "hardly to be found in Irish poetry outside W. B. Yeats, a sort of impersonal *poesie pure,* each poem creating its own universe of images not derived from any occasion nor tied to any particular situation" (Davie 1957, 47–49).

Lips and tongue
wrestle the delicious
    life out of you.

A last drop.
Wonderful.
    A moment's rest.

In the firelight glow
the flickering
    shadows softly

come and go up on the shelf:
red heart and black spade
    hid in the kitchen dark.

Woman throat song
help my head
    back to you sweet.
                    (*NLD*, 13)

It is not the Proust-like revival of one experience by another that is noteworthy here, but the way the images assemble meaning as the poem
unfolds. The *tongue* recurs, for example, in the image of the lamp burning
in the shop where the boy goes to get a sweet from his grandmother:

She was settling the lamp.
Two yellow tongues rose and brightened.
The shop brightened.
                    (*NLD*, 14)

The beady pulp of the pomegranate is anticipated by the "Strings of jet
beads," around the grandmother's neck, and three poems later in the
collection, in "The Tear," it will be casually revealed that the hangings at
the entrance to the grandmother's room are "A fringe of jet drops," which
are visually linked to the title and the subject of the poem itself as well as
to the beads that wreathe the grandmother's neck in "A Hand of Solo."
This poem is not simply recollecting, simply defeating time by naming
over some emotionally charged bit of past experience; rather it aims at a
complicated kind of understanding that goes considerably beyond
Kinsella's early intent merely to stem the passage of time. This is the
collocation of order and understanding Kinsella spoke of in the Haffenden

interview, and it represents the very deep changes in his poetry that the subsequent pages here will pursue: from the stoicism of the early work through the discovery in the poems in *Nightwalker* of a coherence that lifts history above mere anguish, to a radically analytic stance in the late work that explores the growth of consciousness and the very processes of meaning. The changes entail stylistic development from the basically presentative language of the first collections to a profoundly exploratory language in the later work and a change in stance from an observational, externalist pose to the exploration of energizing vision from within. To the extent that Davie's remark about *poesie pure* (see note 8 to this chapter) suggested an independence from "occasion," a power in the poems to spring free of the immediate emotional impact of an event, it was prophetic, as we shall see. Overall the developments to be traced in the chapters to follow here constitute a remarkable and fundamental revolution in Kinsella's poetic, a revolution that opened the way to the comprehensive recuperation of the Irish past and furnished a basis for nothing less than a revivification of contemporary Irish poetry.

1 The Stoic Virtuoso

The seeds of change are present very early on, but what struck many readers of Kinsella's first collections was their remarkable *joie de langue*, a virtuoso verbalism most striking in a beginning poet:

> In hospital where windows meet
> With sunlight in a pleasing feat
>   Of airy architecture
> My love has sweets and grapes to eat,
> The air is like a laundered sheet,
>   The world's a varnished picture.
>   ("A Lady of Quality," *AS*, 7)

From the opening verbal gesture about windows and sunlight to the thin-lipped play on *vanished/varnished* in the last line of this stanza and its companion, "Just for a brittle while," in a subsequent stanza, there is a sense of experience being bent wilfully to specific verbal shape. It is not that the feelings are not "meant," but a kind of Johnsonianism seems to imply that the feelings are validated by the verbal shape, not vice versa.

A similar verbalism informs other poems, such as "Ulysses":

> An orchard, ransacked, its timbers
> Awry in silences,
> Stirs, remembers,
> The superficies
> Of windy disaster, September's
> Little wild miseries
>   (*AS*, 15)

And in "Pause en Route":

> Death, when I am ready, I
> Shall come; drifting where I drown,
> Falling, or by burning, or by
> Sickness, or by striking down.
>
> Nothing you can do can put
> My coming aside, nor what I choose
> To come like—holy, broken or but
> An anonymity—refuse.
>
> (*AS,* 33)

The assonantial play in these extracts we have seen earlier, in the lines from "The Fifth Season." In all of them there is a play on phrasing almost in the musical sense—phrases and clauses that ride across line endings, a series of short lines like "Awry in silences / Stirs, remembers," leading into the contrasting long phrases "The superficies / Of windy disaster, September's / Little wild miseries." In these lines there is moreover a play on tempo in the musical sense, in the shifts from halting phrases like "An orchard, ransacked, . . . Stirs, remembers," into sweeping "melodies" like "September's / Little wild miseries / When briars clawed the path," where the stanza break after *miseries* is overridden into the ambiguously adverbial phrase about the briars. The poems are far from having nothing to say, but they are unquestionably "designed": one younger contemporary of Kinsella's has spoken (not unfavorably) of the "aggressive" formalism of his early work, and the poet himself, speaking of "two voices" in *Another September,* stated that the poems of one of the voices "satisfy a compulsion to arrange rather than to communicate" (Kinsella 1958).

It is instructive in this respect that the visible influences in this early work, and the influences Kinsella himself has asserted, were Yeats and Auden—an Anglo-Irishman and an Englishman—and that the influence never gets deeper than a matter of verbal style. One early poem, "In the Ringwood," from *Another September,* is the baldest possible imitation of Auden:

> As I roved out impatiently
> Good Friday with my bride
> To drink in the rivered Ringwood
> The draughty season's pride

A fell dismay held suddenly
Our feet on the cold hillside.
                                        (*AS*, 37)

Passages that imitate Auden like this, or Yeats, or Eliot ("Ghosts in the afternoon / In agony in the garden"—not Eliot, but Kinsella in "Ulysses") invariably reflect a search for a voice, not necessarily for a vision. This poet (at the time of these poems nearing thirty) has a firmly limited sense of what such acts as poetry can accomplish.

In any case, the order in poetic form as such is unambiguous for the early Kinsella, even if its value or power is not—hence the formal intricacy on which so many of Kinsella's early reviewers commented in such worried tones.[1] Whether he followed the model of Austin Clarke or the practice of ancient Gaelic poetry he had studied on his own, his early assonantial experiments, if we can call them that, issued in intricacies like "Test Case" in *Another September:*

> Readier than flags rippling in the sun
> To turn tragic in elegiac weathers,
> More striking, forked and longer than lightning,
> Is the heroic agenda, full of frightening
> Things to kill or love or level down—
> A man's life, magnified with monumental bothers.
>
> Naked save for the skin of a preferably
> Ferocious beast, pulling down roofs
> Seriously to demonstrate some fact,
> His queer quality is noticed—direct
> Approach, statuesque faith—clearly he
> Is unforgettable. Events will circle him with graves.
>   (*AS*, 3)

Weathers/bothers, sun/down, fact/faith, roofs/graves—these quasi-assonantial pairs stand in logical as well as acoustic relation to each other, and the heroic agenda's turning *tragic in elegiac weathers* is a combination of assonance and irony worthy of *Hugh Selwyn Mauberley.*

---

1. For example, see Ralph Mills's review in *Poetry* (Mills 1969, 273) and Martin Dodsworth in *The Listener* (Dodsworth 1968, 728). Closer to home, Denis Donoghue remarked—in the midst of overall praise—that Kinsella could "learn a good deal [in the way of restraint] from Mr. [Austin] Clarke's *Ancient Lights*, or from the austere poems of Ivor Winters" (Donoghue 1957, 185).

The early poems flaunt a similarly bravura disposition of the long phrase, as in "Baggot Street Deserta," where

> Truth
> Concedes, before the dew, its place
> In the spray of dried forgettings Youth
> Collected when they were a single
> Furious undissected bloom
>
> (*AS*, 30)

and

> I nonetheless inflict, endure,
> Tedium, intracordal hurt,
> The sting of memory's quick, the drear
> Uprooting, burying, prising apart
> Of loves a strident adolescent
> Spent in doubt and vanity.
>
> (*AS*, 31)

"Priest and Emperor" in *Another September* deploys a complex pattern over seven ode-like stanzas of eleven lines each, a pattern where *sternness* as a rhyme word is played off against *harness, torque* against *work*. This collection, like *Downstream* after it, is much committed to regular but complicated stanzaic forms, long and free-wheeling phrases like these two sets playing over firmly designed patterns of lineation and stanza organization. This is true even of so hemmed-in a poem as "Death of a Queen," whose militantly brief lines twice flow beyond any stanzaic containment:

> . . . she came with the step of a goddess,
> Hypocritical, courageous,
> Wreathed with longing, out of the mast
> That crackled under her feet, not with pain
>
> But in pagan accompaniment of applause.
> . . . .
> And she set the fragments under
> And among and up to the boulders' waists
> And watched them fuse,
>
> Forming a body gradually out of the dead.
>
> (*AS*, 2)

The motive for this kind of close control is manifested in the much tidier poem, "An Ancient Ballet." Its Elizabethan neatness—

> In the deep reaches of the night
> The ticking stars keep order
> That when the sleepless border
> On marvel they shall sleep light

—controls the bleakness of what the tidiness seems to gainsay:

> And I think that [the moon's] stare discovers
> Only what we pretend,
> That the moon is lovely, but will descend
> Through the night's honest endeavors.
>
> (*AS*, 18)

"We know," runs a previous line, "her power is our longing." So much for *that* traditionary image. Poetry is not cognition, but at most a buttress against the fragility of human happiness, contentment, even safety. As an activity, it is a search for defenses against entropy and loss.

We've seen Kinsella's remark to an interviewer that his early work was "influenced by literature more than by fact," and the studied formality of poems like the foregoing indeed seems to come out of an intensely literary impulse. But in view of poems like "Baggot Street Deserta" and "Lead," it might be fairer to say that whenever the early Kinsella departs from a certain kind of conventional lyric, a powerful skepticism sets strong boundaries between mind and matter or mind and world. In much of this early work, that is, he calls into question one of the major principles of modernist literature, the assumption that mind can capture in language any such thing as the deep Forms of history or reality. As with much other postmodernist work, the impenetrable wall that is the real drives the Kinsellan mind back upon itself. The mind can only register and react, searching not for any Real beyond what is seen, but essentially for an ethical stance toward what seems to be. Even such poems as "A Lady of Quality," which refers to the poet's visits to the bedside of Eleanor Walsh when she was recovering from tuberculosis, are marked by a grim sense of mortal limit that seems all but primary in the poem: "The ever-present crack in time," which the Lady's behavior attempts to conceal from the speaker, means that " 'Ended and done with' never ceases," and though "We may regret," we can merely "abide." (*AS*, 7). The view of life here is grim enough, but the stance of "Baggot Street Deserta," which is clearly something of an *ars poetica,* is more significant. Looking out upon Reality, again, the poet finds "[its] privacy complete": the only transcendent value, such as it is, available to the poem—or, for that matter, to the poetic act —is the form furnished by the poem; this form is *the* order snatched from decay. Bad or painful as things may be, the poet can make ordered verbal responses to situations, and that order is value. Hypothetical triumph of this sort, however, is pretty slender reward; it leaves things, including the poet, basically unchanged and beyond a rather narrow range renders the poetic act largely ineffectual—at best ad hoc, at worst illusion.

By and large, Kinsella was well served by his early reviewers in Ireland, some of whom saw broader possibilities behind what I have been describing as a bounded sense of the art of poetry. Images like "the ever-present crack in time" in "A Lady of Quality" and "In the deep reaches of the night / The ticking stars keep order" bespeak—even in poems that focus on the idea of human and artistic limitation—at least a yearning awareness of dimensions beyond the human doomed. A very journalistic review of *Another September* (almost in the style of Leopold Bloom) in the *Civil Service Review* included the remark that Kinsella shares to the full the "cosmic vision" of the "extrovert school of modern poetry," and observes that "One can come to understand life as easily in the microcosm as in the planet" ("K.G." 1958, 79). And Peter Levi, reviewing the separate publication of the sequence *Moralities* in a later number of the same journal, remarks that "the pub, the lecture-room or study, the garden and the sea, are not in these poems the horizons of human experience, but simply that hermit's cell of everyday images in which the poet meditates his language and fines it down" (Levi 1960, 269). It would not be long before the potentialities these reviewers claimed to see began to be realized.

Whether or not the bravura performances in *Another September* really parade formal intricacy for its own sake, things became considerably different during the four or so years that produced the poems in Kinsella's next major collection, *Downstream;* here that same formal preoccupation explores and articulates issues much larger than the personal. The poet is clearly pursuing an ambiguously analytic—and modernist—aim to uncover the moral bearings of events by the appropriate disposition of language—which is to say that the formal moves are not so much at the service of the depiction of experience as they are aimed at the revelation of an ethics.

Developing the tendency adumbrated in *Another September* by "Baggot Street Deserta" to build collections out of a kind of tension between short lyrics and longer meditative work, the two long poems in *Down-stream* assert the possibility of a more empowered sense of human and poetic will than Kinsella's first work seemed to concern itself with. Both meditations, "A Country Walk" and "Downstream," brood over history as a chaos of violence and crass self-seeking which, in modern times, has seen the heroic fade into the commercial:

> I came upon the sombre monuments
> That bear their names: MacDonagh & McBride,
> Merchants; Connolly's Commercial Arms. . . .
> ("A Country Walk," *D*, 48)

Not that history ever did offer very much of greater real worth: at the ford the poet passes in "A Country Walk" legend has it that

> There, the day that Christ hung dying, twin
> Brothers armed in hate on either side;
> The day darkened but they moved to meet
> With crossed swords under a dread eclipse
> And mingled their bowels at saga's end.
> There the first Normans massacred my fathers. . . .
> (*D*, 46)

And where antiquity can offer only mindless violence, modern times supply murderous illusion:

> A concrete cross
> Low in the ditch grew to the memory
> Of one who answered latest the phantom hag,
> Tireless Rebellion . . .
> . . . .
> And he lay cold in the Hill Cemetery
> When freedom burned his comrades' itchy palms,
> Too much for flesh and blood, and—armed in hate—
> Brother met brother in a modern light.
> They turned the bloody corner, knelt and killed,
> Who gather still at Easter round his grave,
> Our watchful elders.
> (*D*, 47)

"Civilization" can stem these tides of mayhem? Then how account for "knot-necked Cromwell," who, "with his fervent sword / Despatched a convent shrieking to their Lover"? In any case, civilization as a means of control, as a means of stemming the tide, murderous or otherwise, of entropy, clearly has its limits:

> Joining the two slopes, blocking an ancient way
> With crumbled barracks, castle and brewery
> It took the running river, wrinkling and pouring,
> Into its blunt embrace
>
> (D, 46)

which is to say that civilization, the town, impedes such flow as is natural and might be creative; and the ultimate value of civilization is made plain by the emotional tone of the language:

> Mated, like a fall of rock, with time,
> The place endured its burden: as a froth
> Locked in a swirl of turbulence, a shape
> That forms and fructifies and dies, a wisp
> That hugs the bridge, an omphalos of scraps.
>
> (D, 46)

This town is order of a sort, but then that is probably how Cromwell saw his own depredations, and the whole complex is related to the general failure of political force, that being a major manifestation of what Kinsella has seen as the destructive power of order *imposed*. We see it again in "King John's Castle" in *Another September*. The ruined castle "rams fast down the county of Meath"; once, for a while, "It held speechless under its cold a whole province," but now "The great rooms, the mind of the huge head, are dead," and "Views, lying inward, open on progressive phases of void, / Submarine silence" (AS, 40). *Dead, void, silence:* these are of course not forms of order but the fruits of order imposed, and the theme anticipates Kinsella's later interest in the thinking of C. G. Jung, as we shall see. Of a lesser degree of oppression are those manifestations of imposed order in received rituals such as are observed in "Cover Her Face," a thematically central poem in *Downstream*. Here the meditation essentially dramatizes the failure of conventional forms of order—religion, family, even art—to give shape and meaning to the death of a young woman. Among the mourners who "dither softly at her bedroom door" and those who "make peace, and bite its ashen bread," who understands, the speaker asks, "The sheet pulled white and Maura's locked blue hands?"

And there is no answer. The grim fact of death itself quite dissolves those bonds knit presumably to withstand it:

> a girl they have never seen,
> Sunk now in love and horror to her knees,
> The black official giving discipline
> To shapeless sorrow, these are more their kin,
>
> By grace of breath, than that grave derelict
> Whose blood and feature, like a sleepy host,
> Agreed a while with theirs. . . .
> . . . .
> . . . Such gossamers as hold
> Friends, family—all fortuitous conjunction—
> Sever with bitter whispers; with untold
> Peace shrivel to their anchors in extinction.
>
> (*D*, 22–23)

Many of the poems in *Downstream* address this issue in one form or another. The tentative questioning of "The Laundress" and "Scylla and Charibdis" make it clear that life-forms entail a stifled hunger for what lies outside them. In "Old Harry" imposed order flames in horror; "Harry" is Harry Truman, and the poem is about his ordering the devastation of Hiroshima and Nagasaki:

> Lascivious streets before they shrivelled up
> Heightened their rouge and welcomed baths of pure flame;
> In broad daylight delicate creatures of love
>
> Swayed in a rose illumination of thighs,
> Their breasts melted shyly and bared the white bone;
> At that sight men blushed fiercely and became shades.
> . . . .
> Over the drowsy meadow his favourite
> Martial music struggled with the tea-time breeze;
> Then, whistling a soundless note, he turned for home.
>
> (*D*, 43–44)

We can also see here the fruits of that early virtuosity that remarks like Denis Donoghue's ("Mr. Kinsella could learn a good deal from . . . the austere poems of Ivor Winters") cautioned against. Lines like those about the thighs and breasts of the victims at Hiroshima, with their uncanny control of slow, agonizing insistence, hold one's agonized attention fiercely upon the details of the atrocity—by means which in earlier poems might have been essentially decorative. One swallow does not make a summer, but the style of "Old Harry" cannot be dismissed as unfunctionally flamboyant.

But "Downstream" is at once deeper and more positive than these poems, including "A Country Walk"—certainly more complicated in its confrontation with the human plight. It is a journey-poem thoroughly in the tradition of its Romantic ancestors, particularly perhaps of *Alastor*. It recounts boating downstream to the ancient monastery at Durrow, like Little Gidding and Tintern Abbey a site at once of devotion and learning but now the repository only of ancient bones. It does not reenact *Alastor's* preoccupation with the fate of the poetic impulse, but it certainly makes use of the Romantically speaking landscape.

Between its appearance in *Downstream* in 1962 and its reappearance in more recent collections, the poem was mercilessly revised. The current version is some twenty-nine stanzas shorter than the original. Inquiries about the reasons for the revisions elicit from the poet indefinite phrases about "excessive" and "overblown"—and studied gazes into the middle distance. The revised form is indeed a good deal more chaste in its diction: "We gave our frail skiff to the hungry stream" became "We thrust forward, swaying both as one," and lines like "We raised the tinkling blades and, thrusting behind / A pliant world, assumed the traveller's mask" are doubtless better off consigned to wherever they went at their excision. But the cutting was not limited to stylistic repair; the newer version is more limited in scope than the original, and it is worthwhile to review the earlier version, for it is a compendium of the thematic concerns of Kinsella's early work.

The poem now begins with an epigraph taken from the early version, and the action proper is seen as resuming after some unspecified interruption—as we see in the original, a temporary landing at some darkling inlet along the outing to Durrow where the speaker steps out of the boat and gazes at the stars. After only five stanzas the newer version reflects on an anecdote of a corpse that was found in the woods some years back, which is to lead immediately into the speaker's remembrance of the Holocaust and the Second World War. But the relative brevity of the revised text centers the poem much more on the evil violence of the war than the original, where the violence is involved in a more inclusive thematic development. There, from the very beginning of the poem, nature itself is rife with overtones of menace. What is now the epigraph came from three stanzas that close the first large movement of the original:

> The gathering shades beginning to deceive,
> Night stole the princely scene. . . .
> . . . .
> Drifting to meet us on the darkening stage
> A pattern shivers; whorling in its place
> Another holds us in a living cage
> And drifts to its reordered phase of grace;
> Was it not so? Stabbing the stream, we grooved
> Bloodvelvet furrows in its pearly face.
>
> (*D*, 51)

Twice more the surroundings are referred to as a vaguely menacing "cage," and the harmless river is seen as "the hungry stream," the current of which at one point sucks the speaker's boat "Through sudden calm into a pit of night." Drowsing swans are met as "a ghost of whiteness" and "a Quiet hiss . . . A soul of white with darkness for a nest." The sensed threat in the natural ambience, in fact, silences the speaker's more naïve impulses toward poetizing. Talking poetry with his companion, the speaker

> chose the silken kings,
>
> Luminous with crisis, epochal men
> Waging among the primal clarities
> Productive war

until "The gathering shades beginning to deceive, / Night stole the princely scene," and he has to put his book away. It is at this point that

> Drifting to meet us on the darkening stage
> A pattern shivers; whorling in its place
> Another holds us in a living cage.

Against the backdrop of that threatening natural world are played out the various manifestations of the human with which the poem is concerned: learning, religion, poetry—and violence. In fact, the central polarity of the poem is posed by the natural universe on the one hand and on the other the movements of consciousness, of which the speaker's account of the experience is only one.

The episode of the abandoned corpse has several functions for the poem beyond leading as it does into the political theme. It is, for one thing, a Wordsworthian lesson in concrete reality:

It seemed that I,
Coming to conscience on that lip of dread,
Still dreamed, impervious to calamity,

Imagining a formal drift of the dead
Stretched calm as effigies on velvet dust,

. . . . . when that story thrust
Pungent horror and an actual mess
Into my very face, and taste I must!
(*D*, 54)

The image of the corpse lying on its back in the wood

Spread-eagled on a rack of leaves, almost
Remembering. It searched among the skies,
Calmly encountering the starry host,

Meeting their silver eyes with silver eyes
—An X of wavering flesh, a skull of flame,
That dimmed in our wake and guttered to a close
(*D*, 55)

is surely a reminiscence of Shelley's Alastor-poet staring at the illusory eyes of the Absolute imaged in the twin tips of the crescent moon in the moments before his death, and the theme here is no less ambitious, the image being a grotesque emblem of the relation of the human to the natural universe. The stars the speaker imagines the corpse gazing at are an ironic commentary on his own sanguine meditation of the stars as an image of possible order earlier in the poem.

I stood on the strange earth and stared aloft,

Urmensch and brute, in glassy unconcern,
Where specks of alien light icily hung
Sprinkled in countless silence—there to learn

How the remote chaotic, far outflung
In glittering waste, may shiver and become
A mesh of order, every jewel strung!
(*D*, 52–53)

Like the blank wall the travelers encounter at the end of the poem, these are ultimately ironic expressions of our separation from an ordered natural universe, of the gulf between the sentient human and imponderable reality. The decomposing body, "Collapsed, half-eaten, like a rotted thrush's," offers a grisly enough vision of the "oneness" of man and nature.

And in a way the vision of the corpse is a direct lesson to the poet as such, who, in the early stanzas, has committed the facile error endemic to art—rendering historic acts of mayhem into the deceptive harmlessness of words ("epochal men / Waging among the primal clarities / Productive war"). Worse: these epochal men, "Spurred by the steely pen / To cleansing or didactic rages . . . Fed the stream in turn and deeper still / Drove its course." Such remarks are a body blow against the morality of poetry itself—certainly against such poetic impulses as can be realized in the outworn language of a latter-day Wordsworth, with its "brimming floods" and its "starry host." These excursions into poetic diction, which Kinsella was concerned to excise from the poem, are another expression of the gulf the poem recognizes; we have the word of Wordsworth himself in the Preface to *Lyrical Ballads* that a principal effect of such language is to preclude mind's contact with any authentic surrounding. But there is another aspect to this issue, and it involves the fourth function of the anecdote of the corpse.

The instances of poetic diction are companion to another occasional feature of Kinsella's early style, the seemingly irrelevant effect—the "Pad of owl and hoot of dog" in "Baggot Street Deserta" and the tricksy "fretful star and twinkling bat" in "Downstream." These may be misfires, but they are not self-indulgences. Both poetic diction and the toying with word order are designed partly to distance, by means of their pert irony, the sensibility from the phenomena and to entwine the narrating consciousness with specifically verbal traditions—in short, to render the experience of things as Kinsella always tends to render it, oriented toward a mind conceived of as separate and apart from the perceived natural object, which is as much as to say that mind and things "in themselves" are to be seen as *quite properly* separated. When "Downstream" modulates into a concern with the political in its gruesome lines about Germany and the horror of World War II, we are confronting an extension of the same issue:

> the soil of other lands
>
> Drank lives that summer with a body thirst
> While nerveless by the European pit
> —Ourselves though seven hundred years accurst—

> We gazed on barren earth obscurely lit
>   By tall chimneys flickering in their pall,
>   The haunt of swinish men—each day a spit
>
> That, turning, sweated war, each night a fall
>   Back to the evil dream where rodents ply,
>   Man-rumped, sow-headed, busy with whip and maul.
>
> (D, 54)

This is, in fact, a vision of a primitive or rudimentary or demonic humanity that has not selved from "nature"—the beastly nature of Goneril and Regan and Caliban—against which, in the poem's central meditation, are to be ranged the more humane manifestations of consciousness. So the gulf between the human and the natural is at once a loss and an enabling—an enabling loss like that presented in the opening paragraphs of Lawrence's *Sons and Lovers,* which depict the preindustrial paradise the loss of which makes possible the very tale itself. The separation between natural and human that parts of the poem seem to lament, then, is meet and proper—an opening, even, for the exercise of possibly creative human energies. Whereas "A Country Walk" essentially canvasses forms or instances of failure, the original version of "Downstream" poises consciousness against the forces of entropy and loss, and its concluding lines constitute a declaration:

>   then impended
>   A wall of ancient stone that turned and bared
>   A varied barrenness as toward its base
>   We glided—blotting heaven as it towered—
>
> Searching the darkness for a landing place.

The principal concept here is *search,* not *barrier,* and the emphasis is reiterated in "Mirror in February." The instances of renewal around the speaker—day, the plowed earth, the awakening trees—evince a renovation not open to him, and he must learn

>   that I have looked my last on youth
>   And little more; for they are not made whole
>   That reach the age of Christ.
>
> (D, 63)

The natural renovation the speaker momentarily seems to envy is brutally undercut by the violence apparently necessary to it, given that the awakening trees, "hacked clean for better bearing, stand defaced / Suffering their brute necessities." But the speaker's "shaven jaw" is only shaven, not hacked clean, and the insistent rhyme *defaced/distaste* is ultimately cancelled by the near-rhyme *grace*—this last an attribute of human beings, not trees:

> And how should the flesh not quail that span for span
> Is mutilated more? In slow distaste
> I fold my towel with what grace I can,
> Not young and not renewable, but man.
>
> (D, 63)

Once again the last word is asserted by the defining consciousness of a human artist, and the separation of man from nature is seen not as a curse, but as a locus of potentiality.

That the issue is a false one, however, a post-Romantic atavism finally irrelevant to Kinsella's thought, was to be one of the major discoveries of his subsequent work. It is true that the stoical limitations of that early work reside in the fact that as Kinsella was then writing, things stubbornly *are,* and the mind can only register and react. And yet it is equally true that even his early work is colored by a force analogous to that which imbues the work of other contemporary Irish writers. For them, Ireland has not been merely home; it has been an historical event, and few events in their verse stand free and uncolored by history. Determinedly nonhistorical and non-Irish as the early Kinsella tried to be,[2] his verse is also colored, but differently. He resembles other Irish poets of his generation in that there are for him no simple issues, no simple experiences, and few truly simple things. For him, however, the complicating factor is not Irishness but mortality. It often seems that his speakers can confront nothing in a pure synchronous light; whatever is either will be or has been different. In the earliest work the change is almost invariably felt as either

---

2. Compare John Jordan's comments on Kinsella (Jordan 1962, 111): "Thomas Kinsella is a Dubliner," he points out, but it doesn't show in the poems. "Nor indeed is there much in his verse to suggest the imaginative claim of any of the numerous masks of Ireland. He looks back, it is true, to late-medieval Ireland and finds materials for cameos. But so far he has shown no signs of participation in the immemorial struggle between sow and farrow." Jordan sees this fact as a point of distinction between Kinsella and such contemporaries as John Montague.

loss or an irony occasioned by the very sense of erosion he would have the poem stem. Nothing comes but it comes laden with the speaker's relentlessly ironic consciousness of illusion, loss, or cost. The irony is rooted in the poet's sense that though phenomena may be wrapped round by human response, the response counts for little in the larger scheme of things: "I —a fact / That may be countered or may not— / Find their privacy complete."

The line that divides this mode of thought from what is evinced in Kinsella's later work, fine but of enormous moment, is healthily weakened in *Downstream*. Later still, things will just *not* be in and of themselves; they are, they "mean," what experience has led the mind to make of them. The earlier stance is reactive and looks to the stability of poetic form for solace. The later is formulative, active, and brings to conscious articulation the house that spirit has built itself to dwell in.

The earlier stance concedes a dualism inimical to the direction in which the poet was moving. Clearly, separation need not be alienation, and in any case union and separation are not the only alternatives—they are obstacles, in fact, to the domiciling of the human spirit that was Kinsella's implicit preoccupation. If the early work is governed indeed by an uneasy opposition of self and surroundings, art and entropy, will and loss, part of what the poet needed even on those terms was a more nearly adequate sense of the self he figured himself as deploying. He needed a form of being-with-the-world other than the bringing of mind into some putatively proper tension with the (wholly external) world around it. In a way, he is here recapitulating this century's early struggles with Positivism, his early work hemmed in by the absence of a respectable alternative to the tyranny of "fact" crudely conceived, his later work developing along liberating lines similar to those laid down by the later Wittgenstein and in the assertive speculations of phenomenology.

There was from the outset a specifically Irish force likely to impel him toward a stance considerably more *engagé* than what these early poems generally imply. As my outline of Irish literary tradition makes plain, the Irish poet seems always to have stood in intimate relation with his social audience. Willy-nilly, he or she has been from time immemorial a politically significant figure. Even Yeats—no primitive Gael he—acted out the traditional poet's political role, and this perhaps even at his most aesthetical. Given the Irish literary past (or given Ireland) it would have been unusual for Kinsella to persist in the dualism his early work seemed to take for granted. The point is not that he had inevitably to become political in the usual sense, but that a pull toward *community* that marks the work of many Irish writers strengthened a happily strong impulse to ultimately dislodge himself from the epistemological encapsulation of his early ideas.[3]

An early instrumentality in this process was the recuperative activity of translation, which of course can be seen as bearing "a pull toward community" on its face. In keeping with national policies of the time, Kinsella's primary schooling was in Irish, and one of his first postcollegiate publications was a translation of *Faeth Fiadha* (in English, "The Breastplate of St. Patrick"). He attracted attention with his translation of *Longes Mac n-Usnig* in 1954, and *Thirty-Three Triads* in the year following.[4] These translations, with all their implications of meaningful cultural recuperation, may seem (especially in light of the ideas in "The Irish Writer") to have lain dormant for some years while the poet's *rapprochement* between mind and circumstance, mind and fact, poem and history, gradually developed. But a review by Austin Clarke of Kinsella's *Poems* of 1956 drew a straight line between the "toughness" of Kinsella's language and a familiarity with Irish. More interesting still, the reviewer saw Kinsella's easy transitions from "factual" to imaginative content as the fruit of contact with the Irish literary heritage ("A.C." 1956).[5] In any case, it might be that adequate translation can make possible to some extent the bridging of the terrible gap between living poet and nurturing past. If so, it might be conceivable that consciousness is not irretrievably confined to the powerless roles of perception and response, but on the contrary is able to enter into, and by its own exertions revivify, the heretofore closed life of the past.

Translation in general was to play an important role in a congeries of intellectual and verbal developments that would revolutionize Kinsella's work. Though that revolutionizing came more fully in *Nightwalker and Other Poems* and deepened definitively in *Song of the Night* and *Notes from the Land of the Dead,* the revisions in the current version of the early

3. In appealing to the concept of community here, I am drawing on work by one of Kinsella's best recent critics, W. J. McCormack (McCormack 1987). The pertinence of his concepts to my discussion of Kinsella's later work will be obvious and crucial.

4. See Pearse Hutchinson's enthusiastic review of *Longes Mac n-Usnech* (Hutchinson 1955). The translations in question were all separate publications by Dolmen.

5. For the bearing of this, compare the remark of Proinsias MacCana (MacCana 1970, 55):

[T]he Celtic idea of the otherworld, as this is realised in the literature, allowed a remarkable imaginative fluidity with the natural and supernatural seeming continually to merge and commingle in an almost free variation, and it is perhaps in this light that one should view the regular and easy interchange of zoomorphic and anthropomorphic images.

"King John's Castle" are a dramatic demonstration of Kinsella's ultimate direction. This poem was not pruned so radically as "Downstream," but its revisions actually run deeper. The seven-line stanza of the version in *Another September* has been altered to six lines, in the service of a much bolder intellectual stance. The first stanza of the early version ended

> New, a brute bright plateau,
> A crowded keep plunging like a bolt at Boyne water,
> It held speechless under its cold a whole province of Meath.
>
> (*AS*, 40)

and the second stanza continued, with concession to detail helping disarrange the rhythm,

> Now the spiral stairs, man-rot of passages,
> Broken window-casements coloured with rubbed sandstone,
> Vertical drops chuting through three stories of masonry,
> Are a labyrinth in the medieval dark. There, peering behind them,
> Intriguers foundered into the arms of their own monster.
> There still a spirit visits, with nothing in its embrace,
> The floors of its own mildness fallen through to dust.

The corresponding lines in the version for *Poems 1956–1973* are

> New, a brute bright plateau,
> It held speechless under its cold a whole province of Meath.
>
> Now the man-rot of passages and broken window-casements,
> Vertical drops chuting through three storeys of masonry,
> Draughty spiral stairways loosening in the depths,
> Are a labyrinth in the medieval dark. Intriguers
> Who prowled here once into the waiting arms
> Of their own monster, revisit the blowing dust.
>
> (*P*, 31)

The doubtless real but superfluous color of the casements and the "peering" of the intriguers (by no means real, merely surmised)—these are gone along with the visiting spirit "with nothing in its embrace, / The floors of its own mildness fallen through to dust," this latter concern taken care of in the more compacted language about the intriguers. In the third stanza, "Views, lying inward, open on progressing phases of void, / Submarine silence" becomes in the later version, "Views open inward / On empty silence; a chapel-shelf, moss-grown, unreachable." This is probably the most powerful change of all; in rejecting the original concession to earnest overpresentation, the poem gains enormously in the dramatic authority of its rhythm. The revisions bespeak greater confidence in metaphor and less worried impulsion to name every physical item in the scene. Less is conceded altogether to the representation of factual details apparently felt in the earlier version to be essential to the picture, a picture that scrupulously acknowledges the boundary between mind and its conclusions or assessments on the one hand, and scene and its supposedly irremovable facts on the other. In the revised version mind asserts its vigorous cognitive instrument, language, to perform a confident reduction, which is not reductive, of the scene to its phenomenological significance. This is a move far beyond any simple or stoic opposition of self to surroundings. *Nightwalker*—particularly in "Phoenix Park" and the title poem—shows this move in the process of developing.

2   Turning Point

By the time of Kinsella's next major collection, *Nightwalker,* he had gone through turning points literary, semiliterary, and nonliterary, though given his developing poetics, categorizing is arbitrary. The year after the publication of *Downstream* he had taken a leave of absence from his job with the Finance Department, and though he had no thought then of staying away permanently, a whole year free for the writing of poetry was food for thought.[1] In 1965 (by now a member of the Irish Academy of Letters and recipient of the Dennis Devlin Memorial Award for *Wormwood*) he joined the faculty of Southern Illinois University at Carbondale as poet-in-residence. Henceforth the role of Ireland's leading poet would require full-time work. His marriage with Eleanor Walsh was now a relationship of ten years' standing, and there were children.

All this must have conduced to—it certainly coincided with—an importantly altering sense of the value and possibilities of poetry. Marriage and family had clearly been a locus of struggle; they formed the background and subject matter of *Wormwood,* an important interim collection incorporated into *Nightwalker and Other Poems,* and it is tempting to see there the origin of the poet's concept of *ordeal.* Part of his commentary on *Nightwalker and Other Poems* was that "The first two sections of the

---

1. The circumstances of this leave confer a certain ambiguity on the sense of the poet's isolation and irrelevance that colors Kinsella's early work. A leave of such a length would probably have to have the approval of T. K. Whitaker, the very highly placed civil servant who was Kinsella's ultimate superior, and it says something about the status of serious writers in the Irish Civil Service that the leave was granted at all. By this time in his bureaucratic career, Kinsella was already well along in terms of advancement; more than a few of his contemporary coequals went on to responsible and significant positions in the Civil Service. There is the further fact, remarked on in the previous chapter, of the Service's hospitality to civil servants who entertained commitment to serious writing.

book begin with certain private experiences under the ordeal, and follow with celebrations of countermoves—love, the artistic act—which mitigate the ordeal and make it fruitful, and even promise a bare possibility of order" (Dawe 1987, 28, quoting Kinsella 1967).

The concept is central in the Prologue to the *Wormwood* section:

> It is certain that maturity and peace are to be sought through ordeal after ordeal. . . . We reach out after each new beginning, penetrating our context to know ourselves, and our knowledge increases until we recognize again (more profoundly each time) our pain, indignity and triviality. . . . But if we drink the bitterness and can transmute it and continue, we resume in candour and doubt the only individual joy—the restored necessity to learn. (*N*, 23)

The aims, or hopes, here remain relatively modest—relative, at least, to the conceptions of the generation of Joyce, Pound, and Williams. Note, moreover, that in all of these statements about his own work or about poetry in general, nothing is asserted about the power of language as such. Poetry is assimilated to a general behavior, so to speak, and seems to be seen primarily as structure building; language is regarded almost exclusively for its role in "form": we are far removed here from Pound's or Williams's—or Joyce's—active sense of language as a respository of energy or culture. Nonetheless *Nightwalker* as a whole, and especially the three major poems that make up its fourth section, "Nightwalker," "Ritual of Departure," and "Phoenix Park," promise—even manifest—a revision of the various kinds of isolation that had been characteristic of Thomas Kinsella's poetry and of Thomas Kinsella the poet. His early emulation of Auden, stepping over the literary models of his own country, was formalist in both effect and implication and served to underscore the boundedness of the Kinsellan poet. *Nightwalker* presupposes a far different conception of the poet, and its turn to Joyce in "Nightwalker" was concomitant with a changed sense of what poetry could concern itself with and do.

The talk of ordeal is in itself a new note in Kinsella's thematic commentaries, and the poems in *Nightwalker and Other Poems* center in part on authentic and inauthentic modes of facing ordeals of one kind or another. As with the turn to Joyce, what this means is that Kinsella's work is turning more purposively outward.

Neither *Nightwalker* nor *Nightwalker and Other Poems* is a fully composed book such as Kinsella would undertake in the work that followed them, but apart from the reprinting of some of the poems in *Downstream*

as part 5, its separate sections constitute a purposeful design. It is clear
that "Our Mother," placed first in the volume, is exactly where it ought to
be in relation to the rest of the collection. Standing with his wife at the
bedside of their convalescing daughter and another patient—"All three
women, two in my care, / The third beyond all care, in tears"—the
speaker-poet is clearly staring at a responsibility undefined but real: "Living, dying, I meet their stare / Everywhere, and cannot move" (*N*, 3). The
change in these poems is from the stance of the isolated observer to that
of the troubled participant. What is developing is a tendency that would
be greatly strengthened by Kinsella's discovery of William Carlos Williams, among other influences: the conviction that the "actual" must be
lived, not just observed or accurately represented, and in day-to-day life
certainly not accepted in conformity to some authoritarian fiat. Consider
the instructive contrast between "Office for the Dead" in *Nightwalker*
and "Cover Her Face," from *Downstream*. The earlier poem really is as
descriptive as the later one seems to be, recording in that early Kinsellan
manner the glum truth of how death severs even the ethical ties that link
living people:

> Such gossamers as hold
> Friends, family—all fortuitous conjunction —
> Sever with bitter whispers; with untold
> Peace shrivel to their anchors in extinction.
> There, newly trembling, others grope for function.
>   (*D*, 23)

It is close enough to truth to say that the wan sentence that concludes the
poem, "So we die," sums up its essential stance. The poem in itself seems
called upon to perform an intolerably massive duty—to rescue, by its mere
formal symmetry, the gloomy event from oblivion, to stand, with only its
achieved shape for evidence, as the response of consciousness to entropy
and loss.

The very title of *Nightwalker*'s "Office for the Dead" asserts a more
actively creative human will; the poet's own structures dislodge the institu-
tional discourse of "the grief chewers." The old woman's dying he can do
nothing about, but he can certainly take a position on the inadequacy of
the standard forms to just this case, remarking how "Back and forth, each
side in nasal unison / Against the other, their voices grind across her
body," as "We watch, kneeling like children, and shrink as their Church /
Latin chews our different losses into one" (*N*, 5). As for the other trap-
pings of the standard rite:

> *Sanctus.* We listen with bowed heads to the thrash of chains
> Measuring the silence. The pot gasps in its smoke.
> An animal of metal, dragging itself and breathing . . .

This clearly judgmental imagery places the poet in a stance different from
that of the earlier poem. There is plenty of judgmentalism in "Country
Walk," of course; the poet has his own ideas about the bloody lessons of
history. But *Nightwalker* is a volume of poems much more alive to operations of mind beyond reactive judgment; position taking is not enough,
and much gets said in these poems about attempts of the mind to make
sense of time's inevitable loss, just as much gets demonstrated concerning
the powers of language in particular in those attempts. In poems like
"Traveller," "The Shoals Returning," "Ballydavid Pier," and even "Museum" we are launched into an analytic mode of thought unlike almost
anything in Kinsella's preceding work.

In its pursuit of meaning or understanding, "Ballydavid Pier" is a
skewed "Ode on a Grecian Urn" though it confronts a natural scene rather
than a work of art:

> Noon. The luminous tide
> Climbs through the heat, covering
> Grey shingle. A film of scum
> Searches first among litter,
> Cloudy with (I remember)
> Life; then crystal-clear shallows
> Cool on the stones, silent
> With shells and claws, white fish bones;
> Farther out a bag of flesh,
> Foetus of goat or sheep,
> Wavers below the surface.
>
> Allegory forms of itself
>
> (*N*, 6)

Thou still unravish'd bride of quietness indeed! And there is a query—a
quest, even:

> Small monster of true flesh
> Brought forth somewhere
> In bloody confusion and error
> And flung into bitterness,
> Blood washed white:
> Does that structure satisfy?

No mere emblem here of the outrageous rot Time relentlessly throws up, the polluted waters of the harbor tease the mind out of itself and tug it toward a possibility of meaning, the implied futility of conventional rites and symbols notwithstanding.

For one thing, the speaker is moved by these repellent images of garbage to an all but unexpressed—and surely unexpected—pity:

> The ghost tissue hangs unresisting
> In allegorical waters,
> Lost in self-search
> —A swollen blind brow
> Humbly crumpled over
> Budding limbs, unshaken
> By the spasms of birth or death.

The irony of *allegorical* here is not quite the sardonic irony of earlier poems, for what makes *waters* allegorical is the considering mind of the narrator. The awareness in the last three lines of the agony in life and death is imbued with a warmth of feeling not typical of Kinsella's two earliest collections—perhaps even a *mode* of feeling: consider the difference in the relationship of mind to scene if *humbly* were altered to *horribly*.

The final stanza of the poem reads curiously like the beginning of something, not an end:

> The Angelus. Faint bell-notes
> From some church in the distance
> Tremble over the water.
> It is nothing. The vacant harbour
> Is filling; it will empty.
> The misbirth touches the surface
> And glistens like quicksilver.

The tone of the middle lines of this stanza is not the tone they would have had in *Another September,* and the suggestivity of the final two lines seems rife with possible meaning. There is something beyond stoicism here.

Though the humorous irony of "Museum," on the other hand, looks like more position taking, it really is something more. At every point where it seems about to settle like the museum itself into a single mood, the poem reverses itself. True, the ponderous stones of which the building is made seem a ready-made image of the deadliness of imposed order: "The great Museum / Squats closer on its hoard and will not move." Its "blocks of granite, speechless with fatigue" (*N*, 9), promise to imply inertia and dead weight; but what they balance turns out to be "the slithering pit," the "shapelessly- / Adjusting matter of the rubbish heap," and the complex ambiguity of Kinsella's description of the interior would be hard to summarize:

> Webs of corridors and numbered rooms
> Catch the onward turbulence of forms
> Against museum technique; flux disperses
> In order everywhere.
>
> (*N,* 9)

The temptation to regret imposed order here must be tempered by an awareness of how firmly this set of lines is organized about a very regular, and regulated, pentameter foundation. And who will say whether the order evinced in a museum is imposed or educed? Would the mind prefer the slithering pit of free vitality to the glass cases? The unintelligible exuberance of tongues to the Pauline order of coherent prophecy?

In both of these poems the issue of value has come up in a perspective new to Kinsella's work. Their foundation—we might say the ethical initiative—is laid by "Traveller" (*N,* 15). This poem opens with the speaker at the beginning of a long journey to the bedside of his sick wife, his children "left asleep / In their strange bed." For whatever reason—worry, concentration, the darkness on either side of the road—the speaker's mind turns obsessively inward: "the traps of self / Are open for eighty solitary miles ahead, / In the swerving ditch, in the flash of tree-trunks and hedges." That is to say, every aspect of the fleeting landscape is part of a perception that turns the mind back upon itself, and for what must be the first time in Kinsella's work, the sense of resentful irony, a sense of threat and entrapment, is targeted not on the exterior world or on history, but on the self:

> The brain, woken to itself and restless,
> Senses their black mouths muttering in the darkness:
> Phrases, echoes of feeling, from other journeys
> To bait and confuse the predatory will
> And draw it aside, muttering in absent response,
> Down stale paths in the dark to a stale lair,
> In brainless trance, where it can treadle and chew
> Old pangs blunter and smoother, old self-mutilations.
>
> (*N,* 15)

For the moment this is Lawrentian man, a solipsistic will at the controls of a machine, plunging through a solipsistically read darkness it is using to reinforce its own obsessive self-orientation, engaged in the only nonme-

chanical activity open to the post-Lockean mind, the meditation of inner
states, inner hurts. The unfamiliar, the dark, is felt exclusively as threat. Yet
light is light, and "Far ahead on the road the lamps caught something."

> It rose slowly, white furred, and flew
> Up into the dark. An owl! My heart
> Stood still. I had forgotten the very existence.
>   (*N*, 15)

The illumination (itself purely mechanical, we may note) draws the poet
perforce out of himself, out of those solipsistic traps posed by the self-
preoccupied brain, and toward, it may be, the kind of meditation that
occupies "Ballydavid Pier"—certainly to the awareness that there *is* something "out there," something ("A cat. A bird. . . . An owl!") the mind has
to bestir itself to recognize, something that calls the mind to discrimina-
tions not purely subjective.

The triangulation these three poems perform manifests a cluster of
ambitious new concerns. "Museum" presses an underlying epistemology,
putting the question of whether the act of knowing entails a deceptive and
illegitimate imposition of arbitrary and life-denying order on vital process
or in fact *educes* order and confers life-enhancing stability on the seeming
decay of time-bound phenomena. "Ballydavid Pier" canvasses the very
possibility of meaningful knowledge, and "Traveller" dramatizes a galva-
nizing of consciousness that is fundamental to the other two acts of meditation. Clearly, discussion has come to involve a level of critical language
not called up by the poems in Kinsella's first collections.

It does not slight the earlier poems to say that these three show the
mind engaging with its surroundings in a more complicated way than was
characteristic of either *Another September* or *Downstream*, and in the three
major poems that make up the concluding part 4 of *Nightwalker*, "The
Shoals Returning," "Nightwalker," and "Phoenix Park," the distance
Kinsella has come amounts almost to a new poetics.

The analytic bent, so to call it, of "The Shoals Returning" (*N*, 33–38)
radically revises the more blunted and finally abandoned attempt in the
images of "Baggot Street Deserta" to propose a link between the actions
of the poet and both his community and the surrounding natural ambience, and it similarly revises the imperfect gestures of "Downstream" toward allegorizing the moves of the poet. Poised in a rowboat on the sea,
the speaker is moved to a long meditation on the life and fate of the
fisherman whose death is the chief focus of the poem. The ambiguous

language that presents the speaker in his boat, "supported and opposed" on the "green flesh of the wave," is reminiscent of the ambiguity in the imagery of "Downstream," and the abrupt, blunt introduction of the death recalls the corpse in the earlier poem; here "A corpse balanced among / Striped fathoms turns / Over face upward." The solitary corpse in "Downstream" has a "significance" that is moral *tout court,* if it has any significance at all; one of the applications of that grisly exemplum is to remind the speaker of the brute reality of death as a condition to be confronted. In "The Shoals Returning" death is rather a problem to be weighed, and as this poem moves from vignette to vignette, the mind of the poem is everywhere conscious of the pertinence of the events and personages to the activities of the poet himself:

> Nets are shaken out
> And swallowed into the sea.
> The lines reach far down
> And open everywhere
> Among the haunted levels.
> A million shadows
> Pursue their staring will
> Along echoing cold paths.
>   (N, 37)

Sinking nets of lines that reach far down is certainly one figure for the poet's own task, and the singing of the doomed fisherman is another:

> In the exercise of his gift
> His throat constricts; speech,
> Human proportion, distort
> Slightly to permit the cry
> That can prepare the spirit
> To turn softly and be eaten
> In the smell of brine and blood.
>   (N, 35)

It is obvious enough that the language here implies a deep linkage between the significance of priestly discourse, poetry, and the fisherman's casual song—but we would not have found such a linkage proposed in the earlier collections. Like a poet's (it is to be hoped), this song also "articulates and pierces," and the sea on which the fisherman moves in pursuit of his calling is as much a landscape as anything we have seen Kinsella explore. The fishermen

> move out with crisp
> Tangles of net, vague
> Oar-voices, a fading
> Taint of canvas and rope.
> Past cliff wall and washed rocks
> Over meshes of hissing foam.
> They cross into the Sound
> And climb the swell blindly,
> Dropping in dark valleys.
>
> (*N*, 36)

It needs no laboring that fisherman and poet alike are in intimate touch
with deep symbolic and dangerous forces, and that the appropriate taking
up of a natural "prosperity"—here, the return of the mackerel after some
lean years—entails departure into danger:

> In that Autumn, after fifteen
> Years, a new direction
> Loosened the seed in the depths;
> The mackerel shoals reappeared
> And the water in the Sound shivered.
>
> (*N*, 35)

The fisherman who suffers the fate of his catch has run the risk for which
the poet's risk is a figure. It is crucial to the one profession as to the other
not to sink into the shapeless ambience containing and concealing the
necessary sustenance of each. Again, in a description of netted fish we
confront one version of the relation between the poetic mind and the
living reality it must codify—in short, the ambiguity of "Museum," only
here not comic:

> The delicate veil of garottes
> Drags, scarcely breathing,
> Then touches a living shoal.
> Fierce bodies leap into being
> Strangling all over the net,
> An anguish of shivering lives.
> They gather weight, shudder
> By shudder, and—gazing about them—
> Turn to unbearable stone.
>
> (*N*, 37)

In this poem we have not two entities, surroundings containing certain things and a consciousness trying to decide how to feel about them,

but a complex unity, an intertwining of subject and object that echo each other, share a set of terms *(net, sing, catch, constrict, drop in dark valleys)* and therefore to some extent share an identity. Here Kinsella is writing in terms of a profound Romanticism he could only imitate stylistically in "Downstream," where his Wordsworthianism was a matter of "brimming floods" and suchlike, and where the story line was a convenient device on which to hang his moral musings. Is the fisherman a figure for the poet, or is the poet a figure for the fisherman? Kinsella is here entering on work that renders such questions impertinent. He has moved to a discourse not at all Wordsworthian in style but deeply so in its vision of the analogies between the operations of the poetic mind and the events elsewhere, and the "plot" has become a cluster of meaning-laden episodes not strung factitiously along a story line but simply thought about. This poem does not just take a stance toward death; approximating the Wittgensteinian conception of *knowing* as *seeing-as,* it asks how the mind can best make sense of what it looks upon. The very function of imagery has changed, from description, however complex, to synthesis.

Notwithstanding its seeming retreat from the epistemological focus of the foregoing poems to a focus on the explicitly ethical, "Nightwalker" manifests a no less far-reaching advance in the development of Kinsella's poetics. It covers some of the same ground as "Country Walk" but with important differences. Like that earlier poem, like "Downstream," and like "Phoenix Park," it makes use of the set journey, but this time the convention is touched by the example of Joyce, which like the touch of a wand seems to dissolve familiar methods into magical new ways. It reads in part like a "Rhapsody on a Windy Night" empowered by a Joycean dissolution of the narrative self (and in this sense, then, it also resembles *The Waste Land,* whose narrator, like Joyce's, disappears into voices that constitute parts of the poem). Unquestionably, something new is going on with Kinsella's sense of how to structure a poem and with his sense of the self, both the poetic self and the self as participant in events.

For one thing, "Nightwalker" works with a much larger measure of personal responsibility than either "A Country Walk" or "Downstream." The mood of "A Country Walk" is stoically limited; history is violence, mankind unregenerately violent, but no one is really to blame, and all the poet can do about it is to arrive at ordered structurings of his own perceptions of all that. Accordingly, there are legends and legendary figures in "A Country Walk" but no persons. In "Nightwalker" there are indeed persons, persons emerging into legendary status: the giant creators, Joyce and Yeats, and the bestial destroyers, De Valera, O'Higgins, and their political ilk. The difference can seem almost programmatic, but it is importantly linked with the difference between his early view that the function of poetry is to stem the tide of loss by the erection of forms and the comments in that 1967 statement in the Poetry Society *Bulletin* to the effect that the poems in *Nightwalker* had as their subject in general "a developing view of life as ordeal." Ten years later he was still finding that term appropriate: "One is presented with a lifespan which manifests itself largely as ordeal, stages through which one is tested more and more deeply," and he went on, "an awareness of life as an ordeal will lead inevitably, in a certain temperament, to an artistic response, an attempt to hold things in place" (Haffenden 1981, 102). *Ordeal, test:* such terms imply the possibility of coherence or meaningfulness. Thus order in "Museum" is a subject for speculation and assessment, whereas earlier it might have been only the desideratum of a wistful nostalgia. And so with the references to concrete persons in "Nightwalker." Where "Downstream" gives a generalized, mythlike version of German atrocity, "Nightwalker" gives

> Bruder und Schwester
> —Two young Germans I had in this morning
> Wanting to transfer investment income;
> The sister a business figurehead, her brother
> Otterfaced, with exasperated smiles
> . . . .
> I cannot take
> My eyes from their pallor. A red glare
> Plays on their faces, livid with little splashes
> Of blazing fat. The oven door closes.
>
> (*N*, 58)

Where "A Country Walk" has references to fraternal slaughter seen through the edgeless lens of legend, "Nightwalker" has a rumination on modern murderousness barely distanced by an ironic popular myth of De Valera, Kevin O'Higgins, and Rory O'Connor:

> Look! The Wedding Group:
> The Groom, the Best Man, the Fox, and their three ladies
> —A tragic tale: soon, the story tells,
> Enmity sprang up between them, and the Fox
> Took to the wilds. Then, to the Groom's sorrow,
> His dear friend left him also, vowing hatred.
> So they began destroying the Groom's substance
> And he sent out to hunt the Fox, but trapped

His friend instead; mourning, he slaughtered him.
Shortly, in his turn, the Groom was savaged
On a Sunday morning, no one knows by whom
(Though it's known the Fox is a friend of Death and rues Nothing).
                                                    (*N*, 59) [2]

Both examples participate in the speaker's conviction that an all-con-
suming necrophilia lies at the core of the decay and failure the poem
records—the necropolist blue glare of television screens ("bodies move /
Obliquely and stoop, flickering—embalmers / In eery light underground")
is recalled in the pallor of the two Germans; the death-obsession of Fox
and friends is anticipated in the speaker's musings about "the ministers"
—participant-survivors of the bloody internecine warfare that followed
independence—who function so well because "the blood of enemies /
And brothers dried on their hide long ago"; they are "Shadow-flesh. . .
claimed by pattern still living, / Linked into constellations with their
dead." This, to be sure, is position taking, but again there is some possibility of understanding in a world where, as Ezra Pound once put it, politicians have last names and addresses.

It was suggested in the previous chapter that in the days when
Kinsella was emulating the tones of Auden and Yeats, he was seeking a
voice rather than a vision. In "Nightwalker" voice is deployed to embody
vision and becomes an aspect of structure. With Joycean zest Kinsella
dissolves his narrator's consciousness into a tragicomic series of contrasting voices—Joyce, for one:

Subjects will find
The going hard but rewarding. You may give offence
But this should pass. Marry the Boss's daughter.
                                                    (*N*, 62)

And in the seedy discourse of "Brother Burke," a schoolteacher-priest, he
can use language to embody the death of language and expose the militant

---

2. The Groom was Kevin O'Higgins; the Best Man, Rory O'Connor; and the Fox, of
course, Eamon De Valera. The three were colleagues in the struggle for Irish independence,
but O'Connor was among the anti-Treaty men (i.e., Republicans) who occupied the Four
Courts in April 1922, and was one of the four executed on orders approved by the Groom,
Kevin O'Higgins. Five years later O'Higgins was assassinated on his way to Mass—on
whose orders it is fruitless to ask. An indeterminate outline of the whole affair can be pieced
together from the monumentally discreet remarks in Coogan 1966, where, according to
W. J. MacCormack, Kinsella probably saw the photograph referred to in the poem. The
account in Kee 1972 (vol. 3, chap. 12) is more detailed and might be more informative for
readers less familiar with the history of the Free State.

necrophilia of a down-at-heels religiosity that subverts even education for
the benefit of a de-energized politico-theological agenda:

> . . . the authorities
> Used the National Schools to try to conquer
> The Irish national spirit, at the same time
> Exterminating what they called our "jargon"
> —The Irish language; in which Saint Patrick, Saint Bridget
> And Saint Columcille taught and prayed!
> Edmund Ignatius Rice founded our Order
> . . . .
> the present Taoisach
> Sat where one of you is sitting now.
>
> (N, 63–64)

The poem, then, renders up an ordered picture built around perceptions of disorder, and its focal point is not the mere "aesthetic" order of
the poem as such, but the informed moral awareness of the overall discourse. And it perhaps goes some way toward giving a poetic body to
Kinsella's conceptual *bête noir,* order imposed, which is what all the various public functions he canvasses amount to; it is a translation of the
issues in "King John's Castle" to a pragmatic level a younger Kinsella
perhaps could not have managed. And it presents another application of
the concept of responsibility in Kinsella's developing poetics. In using
specific cases and definite persons, he has added the parameter of human
will to his view of evil actions in history. Again, in a universe where things
are done by *persons,* the possibility that the pain of human life may be a
significant, or at least an understandable, ordeal rather than random loss
is considerably stronger. Hence: "I believe now that love is half persistence, / A medium in which, from change to change, / Understanding may
be gathered." What the indeterminate speaker of these lines (their context
is an allusion to Goethe's Werther seeing Charlotte at the window) seems
principally to understand is the moral nature of the phenomena around
him, and that nature is not commendable. In fact, the passage which
asserts that love is "A medium in which, from change to change, / Understanding may be gained" leads directly into some discourse by Queen
Victoria that is morally confused in the extreme:

> It was a terrible time,
> Nothing but sadness and horrors of one kind and another.
> . . . .
> From time to time it seems that everything
> Is breaking down; but we must never despair.

There are times it is all a meaningful drama

· ·

· · · · · reaching through the years to unknown goals
In the consciousness of man, which is very soothing.

(N, 66)

The marvelously flaccid rhythms of this passage match its moral tone to perfection. (How far Kinsella has come from his early need for boundedness is demonstrated by this extending of the poem into actual historical discourse, and discovering therein an expressiveness which is at once risible and all too meaningful.[3] It is against voices like this and like the voice of Brother Burke that the poem asserts his own renderings of the voices of Joyce and Yeats and Goethe—and ultimately the voice of Ireland's legendary Amargin:

> *Alas, I think I will dash myself*
> *At the stones. I will become a wind on the sea*
> *Or a wave of the sea again, or a sea sound.*
> *At the first light of the sun I stirred on my rock;*
> *I have seen the sun go down at the end of the world;*
> *Now I fly across the face of the moon.*
>
> (N, 65)

The speaker's comment on Amargin's declamation uses the very phrase Kinsella used in "The Irish Writer": "A dying language echoes / Across a century's silence." Amargin echoes, of course, in the mind of the speaker-poet, who aligns himself with the voices of poets against the sterile or corrosive voices of the conventional politicians recent history has thrown up. The mind of the authentic poet may be a divided mind, as Kinsella characterizes it in a later version of "The Irish Writer" (Kinsella 1973), but like the division of sexes, it is fruitful, in this case generating a fruitful counterforce against the destructive hegemony of the worldly corrupt. It begins to seem that the voice of poetry can be a force in the world, and not simply the enunciation of a defensive holding force. To be sure, the conclusion of this poem is a bitter one: "In the mind darkness tosses: / . . . / I think this is the Sea of Disappointment." But if that final word is not such as to argue any great wisdom, it may represent the last stage before it. As for the poetry itself, style is clearly coming more and more to embody substance, *voice* has become much more than the striking of an attitude, and mind has come to establish structures that are more

---

3. The passage in question is a pastiche of passages adapted from the diaries of Queen Victoria.

than aesthetic merely. Or is it more accurate to say that in a poem like this one, the concept of the aesthetic has itself undergone a significant invigoration?

Phoenix Park" is an ambitious extension of the kind of poetry embodied in "The Shoals Returning" and "Nightwalker." If the latter poem is pivotal for its invoking the methods of Joyce for the first time in Kinsella's work, "Phoenix Park" is pivotal in several other ways and in terms of Kinsella's development is probably the more significant of the two. For one thing, it has the positive side that "Nightwalker," at least on the surface, has not, moving from Kinsella's earlier insistent consciousness of loss, and of change itself as loss, to the feeling that loss or change can lead to gain or even be a kind of gain. This change is grounded in a second: that move from a sense of meaningless entropy to the notion of meaningful ordeal and a new sense of things—pain included—as a coherent, possibly unitary, structure. This is coordinate with Kinsella's move beyond the brooding lyricism of his earlier work, from an epistemologically bounded lyricism to a claim for the poetic act as conducing to the perception of large-scale pattern, deep and far-reaching significances. This is why "Phoenix Park" seems to either dismiss or radically redefine the phenomenal level that constitutes the chief focus of "Nightwalker." The poem thus consolidates the move from a sense of mind as bounded to a conception of mind empowered that is at work in "Nightwalker." Finally, it adumbrates a new kind of poetic language for Kinsella, reflecting the concept that language possesses something more than the limited and limiting power of ostension. When W. J. McCormack ascribes to the techniques of *Nightwalker* an approximation to allegory (McCormack 1987, 63), he has in mind something that culminates, in Kinsella's later work, in the deployment of a powerful polyvalence. Note, he says of a later poem by Kinsella, how a multitude of possible references "are visibly *there* in the writing, not as several types of ambiguity but as the pluralities of meaning, the layers of palimpsest inevitable in the manifestation of this allegoric opposition to the oneness of Death" (McCormack 1987, 72). This is precisely what was at work, of course, in "The Shoals Returning." The burlesques in "Nightwalker" have signaled the overt onset of this strategy, but even "Ballydavid Pier" and "Museum" foreshadow it. Things now do not stand still in Kinsellan presentations; in a sense different from what the phrase meant in the previous chapter they are and are not. This view is so central to the method of "Phoenix Park" that it is practically the theme.

The poem is a farewell to Dublin—it draws on the Kinsellas' last few days before their departure for Carbondale and Southern Illinois University. Each of its four sections begins with an account of specific moments in a farewell visit to Phoenix Park and modulates (more accurately, the moments dissolve) into a meditative exploration of the spiritual reality of the couple's relationship and their/its surroundings and, to some extent, history. The point of view is firmly that of the narrating poet, who is moved to meditative speech by his wife's observation that he writes her nothing, "no love songs, any more." As he recounts moments in the history of their relationship, the events figure chiefly as experiences of the narrator. The second part, and second stage, is mainly taken up by the poet's expatiation on the noumenal-seeming principles to which he has been led by his beloved, principles couched at this point in relentlessly abstract terms—certain "laws of order," and a subphenomenal "crystal world" that seems to be the metaphysical ground for phenomenal experience. This is followed in a third section by the poet's return to the concretely personal in a condition of informed acceptance and understanding of the "laws of order"; more conscious than heretofore of the moral imperatives of their relationship, he recognizes that to refuse the "ordeal cup" presented by a genuine affectional relationship is to court a condition where "the vivifying eye clouds" and "order dulls and dies in love's death." (This negative possibility gathers up the positive version asserted in the prologue to the *Wormwood* section quoted earlier: "if we drink the bitterness and transmute it and continue, we resume in candor and doubt the only individual joy—the restored necessity to learn.") Finally the transcendent mode of a fourth part sees the couple return physically to the necropolis of history, factual Dublin, but leaves the speaker immersed in his memories of the history of their relationship and its spiritual implications —aware and activated, though groping for an adequate understanding, an adequate rendering, of the emotional materials he has reviewed for his beloved in the course of the poem. And then like "Nightwalker," this poem, too, ends with a suggestive but indeterminate vision:

> A snake out of the void moves in my mouth, sucks
> A triple darkness. A few ancient faces
> Detach and begin to circle. Deeper still
> Delicate distinct tissue begins to form.
>
> (*N*, 84)

The poem is, in fact, an oddly literalized version of the quest-romance: each of its four sections involves departure from a *place* in search of a *condition,* and despite the recurrent focus on the couple's love relationship, the goal of this odd quest emerges as the completion of the speaker's creative self and its empowerment as a poetic potentiality—a bloodless-sounding program so put, but sorting less oddly than might seem with the realistic framework of the couple's farewell to Dublin. The focus on self here is a furtherance of the theme of "Traveller," but there is something additional in the poem's candid pursuit of the noumenal behind the phenomenal details with which the narrating consciousness is so dramatically entwined. A reference to St. Mary's Hospital, for example, where the poet had visited the beloved during her illness, reads in part:

> The Chapelizod Gate. Dense trees on our right,
> Sycamores and chestnuts around the entrance
> To St. Mary's Hospital.
>
> (N, 75)

Considering the possibilities for polyvalence in a stanza (not to mention an urban setting) in which the Chapel of Iseult and a St. Mary's Hospital are near neighbors, a reader can be forgiven for feeling that these two copalimpsests imply some possibly fundamental *tertium quid*. This is to say that "Phoenix Park" claims eventually to penetrate to motivating or seminal principles that inform phenomenal events—the vulnerable detritus of history's aimless flow. In this poem the noumenal takes precedence over the phenomenal, and arrayed about that central pair cluster others: the personal takes precedence over the historical, the intelligibility of ordeal over mere pain, pattern over person.

The primacy of the personal over the historical comes as no surprise after the jaundiced experiences of "Nightwalker"[4] and "A Country Walk." The historical is discredited both by its unremitting mayhem and by its mere perishability as the vehicle of the loss that so imbues the earlier work. Such significance as is discovered in it by Kinsella's early work is not much —partly testimony to ironic transiency, as in "King John's Castle," and partly the limited concretizing of certain abstractions, as with the mysterious corpse in "Downstream." Beyond that, history is essentially the medium in which flounder the vipers and victims of mutability as they drift ever downward to Dis, and its lessons amount to little more than the idea that what happens happens.

---

4. "I pin my hopes," Kinsella wrote of *Nightwalker*, "on the reader's giving due weight . . . to the third part of the waters, in 'Wormwood,' and not all, becoming bitter; on his taking the poem 'Nightwalker' not as political satire or an exile's criticism but as a sad poem about violence, etc." (Kinsella 1967).

The personal, on the other hand, manifests a great deal. The adaptation of language from Crashaw's "In the Holy Nativity of our Lord God," which Carolyn Rosenberg noted (Rosenberg 1980, 222), assimilates the attributes of divinity to the mortal lovers of "Phoenix Park." The epigraph, *The Phoenix builds the Phoenix' nest. / Love's architecture is his own*, asserts the lovers' moral independence vis-à-vis the necropolis of Dublin in the language Crashaw's Chorus applies to the Christ-child, and this miraculous ontological self-sufficiency of the deity (in Crashaw's "We saw thee by thine own sweet light") is again adapted to the lovers—"You approach the centre by its own sweet light"—as is the exalted close of Crashaw's Chorus, "burnt at last in fire of Thy fair eyes, / Ourselves become our own best sacrifice" in Kinsella's exalted quotation near the end of the third part of his poem: *"Our selves become our own best sacrifice. / Continue, so. We'll perish in each other"* (*N*, 82). It might seem plausible to take this assertive arrogation of spiritual power to a specific human love relationship as a further manifestation of the boundedness of the Kinsellan outlook, the mind withdrawing not behind the barriers of poetry but within the pale of human love, and disdaining the world. But the couple's love here is seen as a mode of learning, not a replacement for Fortress Art, but a territory through which runs the path out of isolation to comprehension in all its meanings: "Midsummer, and I had tasted your knowledge, / My flesh blazing in yours; Autumn, / I had learned / Giving without tearing is not possible" (*N, 77*)—what is learned here being a structural principle, so to put it, of human relationships, as in

> And the crystal so increases,
> Eliciting in its substance from the dark
> The slowly forming laws it increases by,
>
> Laws of order I find I have discovered
> Mainly at your hands . . . of failure and increase,
> . . . .
> That life is hunger, hunger is for order,
> And hunger satisfied brings on new hunger
> (*N*, 78–79)

Places and times rendered meaningless by the failures of history (the park itself, for instance, from whose famously murder-tainted past no creditable regrowth ever arose) take on meaning rather from the love of the speaker and "fair Ellinor": "The road divides and we can take either way, / Etcetera. The Phoenix Park; Inchicore, / Passing Phoenix Street . . . the ways are one, sweet choise," opposed to

Return by the mental ways we have ourselves
Established, past visages of memory
Set at every turn: where we smiled and passed
Without a second thought, or stood in the rain
And whispered bitterly; where we roamed at night
(*N*, 83)

On their face, such declarations have only such value as may be, but again the poem is not resting on the conventional valorizing of eros; it is interested not only in sentiment but in furtherance, and the personal here is felt as manifesting deep principles of life.

For a number of implicit dualities shadow the figures of the poet and Eleanor: poet and anima, mind and body, masculine and feminine, all telescoped upon each other. In a curiously tentative blend of literary convention and Jung (by now Kinsella had read and found useful Jolande Jacobi's book on Jungian thought), the feminine is given the role of instructress and, conventionally enough, perhaps, inspiritrice. The entire meditation is prompted in the first place by the woman, and when the poet offers her his expression of the "Laws of order I find I have discovered / Mainly at your hands," he says, "I give them back not as your body knows them . . . But mental, in my fever—mere idea," more or less discounting thus his native mode of apprehension—this at the conclusion of the most abstract section of the whole poem. A series of occasions in the "preparation" for the "one positive dream" he offers at the beginning of the poem, in lieu of the increasingly inadequate lyrical ("Sorry it is not anything for singing") describes the unhoused male's gradual attainment of a wisdom that entails fusion with the flesh and the feminine. Once, he says, "I came alone / To the railings round the Pond, whispered *Take me / I am nothing*," and he is led to recall an emblematic occasion when he encountered "A woman . . . thin and tired," who "interrupted kindly, in vague hunger," and again mind is called into action: "I studied her and saw shame does not matter, / Nor kindness when there's no answering hunger." But the real, the full learning comes from Eleanor, of whom this shadowy Wordsworthian figure is an anticipation. With Eleanor "studying" is replaced by learning and knowledge, the vitalization and enlightenment of mind through its fusion with body:

I found you, in feverish sleep, where you lay.
Midsummer, and I had tasted your knowledge,
My flesh blazing in yours; Autumn, I had learned
Giving without tearing is not possible.
(*N*, 77)

The personages in the poem are also shadowed—and further energized, it may be—by mythic analogies. Conducting the family car up and down the topography of the Dublin necropolis, into and then out of the historical land of death (with its "smoke-soft odour of graves" and its "dead men, / Half hindered by dead men" tearing down "dead beauty" *N*, 82), the poet is surely a mortal Dis—more and more this figure of the poet-speaker as the explorer of two realms will come to punctuate Kinsella's poems, a conceptual extension of the analogy between poet and fisherman in "The Shoals Returning." Both Eleanor and their daughter, Sara, participate in the Persephone figure: "Our first-born," who "stooped in her Communion finery . . . and plucked / Something out of the ground for us to admire," (*N*, 77) is answered in the poet's feeling about her mother when Eleanor "wait[s] a minute on the path, absently . . . tying a flimsy scarf," and "I shiver / Seeing your thoughtless delicate completeness" (*N*, 81).

Such scenes can be read, to be sure, as manifestations of a controlling male gaze, and the Persephone myth as but an unmasking of the aggressive malevolence implicit in that gaze; but Eleanor and the woman who accosts the poet in that educative confrontation with one aspect of the unstructured historical echo manifestations of a powerful feminine principle, which takes many forms in Irish myth, history, and literature—Maebh, Banba, Brigid/St. Brigid, Maud Gonne, Cathleen ni Houlihan, among others (one manifestation made its way into English traditions—the enchanted hag in the tale of the Wife of Bath).[5]

As the fearsome and nourishing Gaea Mater who bestows destruction as readily as life she too will appear repeatedly in Kinsella's later work. Here in "Phoenix Park" her fearsome side is at first barely suggested, by the fever and fire associated with both Eleanor and the street woman: "I found you, in feverish sleep, where you lay. . . . your body's fever leaped

---

5. The figure of the Hag is one source of the feminine metaphors for Ireland that Joyce manipulates in *Ulysses*. The encounter with the woman in "Phoenix Park" is reminiscent of the adventure of young Davin in *A Portrait of the Artist as a Young Man:* soliciting a drink of water at an isolated cottage after dark, he tells Stephen, he was invited to stay the night by the young country wife, whose husband was away. Shying away perhaps from the possibly dangerous supernatural, Davin declined—a refusal ironic enough in this intense spokesman for true Irish ways. In "The Look of a Queen," in Gallagher 1983, Hugh Kenner takes up the deadly side of the Hag in Yeats and Joyce, and in the same collection Maire Cruise O'Brien ("The Female Principle in Gaelic Poetry") writes with great zest and illumination on the positive or creative side. In the same book, Lorna Reynolds gives a stimulating historical account of the figure.

See also Sharkey 1975. As Sheela-na-gig and as Morrighan, the Hag takes on the devouring-mother aspect of Gaea Mater.

out at my mind." And though the wasting fever becomes the fire of the phoenix when the poet succeeds to participation ("My flesh blazing in yours"), the destructive potential is recorded in the speaker's grim reference to the tearing which is the inevitable concomitant of giving.

That Eleanor is an educative force in the speaker's development stirs another mythic resonance. To the extent that the poem turns on the attainment of a proper rapprochement of its various dualities and on the meet articulation of its central relationship, it has analogies with the ancient Irish ritual of union—explicitly sexual—of king and Sovereignty. The *banais,* or wedding feast, was as recently as the fourteenth century a part of the inauguration of the king of Connacht; it was followed by the king's sleeping with the woman who embodied for the occasion the sovereignty of the province.[6] The Irish (or the Celts in general) seem to have bodied forth with uncommon baldness a deep and not often attractive ambivalence about the feminine. Maebh, the great earth mother in the Irish pantheon and transparently a Kali-figure, is by turns nurturing and murderous, and in the Cuchulain legends an ambivalence about woman is embodied in the rivalry of Scathach and Aoife, the hero's foster mother and wife.[7] But the important point is that the union or fusion with the female is enabling—without it the male figure simply does not accede to his full powers; with it, he does. When King Eochaidh commanded a feast at Tara for the purpose of assessing taxes, he was defied by his subjects on the grounds that he had no queen and was therefore no king. Furthermore the sovereignty-goddess apparently enforced possession of kingly virtues; it was for her to say whether the man who would be king was living up to the ethic of his role (MacCana 1970, 120). This echo chamber of Celtic myth, which resounds as well with such things as the relationship of Dante and Beatrice and the significance of feminine figures in a whole string of modernist writers—Yeats, Joyce, Pound, Wil-

6. See Binchy 1970, 11, 12. And cf. Sharkey 1975, 13: "According to Geraldus Cambrensis, the ritual of installing the king included the king's sitting in a broth made from a sacrificial mare, of which he also drinks." Alwyn and Brinley Rees (Rees 1961, chaps. 2, 15) briefly discuss the King-Sovereignty pair in the tales of Niall and Conn. In Dion Boucicault's drama, *Robert Emmet,* the character Sarah Curran is an embodiment of Ireland, according to Maureen S. G. Hawkins: "Emmet regards the eve of his execution as 'the eve of my wedding night. I lie down in my grave to dream of [Sarah] until I wake to meet my bride at the altar of heaven.' As we have seen, that bride proves to be Ireland herself" (Gallagher 1983, 133).

7. Lorna Reynolds (Gallagher 1983, 11–25) furnishes a striking review of the strong women figures in Irish myth and history, including Liadan, a female poet who refused to give up her art in order merely to marry.

liams, Stevens—intensifies, at least conceptually, the significance that can be claimed for the personages in "Phoenix Park." Like the turn implied in Yeats's poetics by poems like "No Second Troy," it marks a willingness to locate some kind of transcendence in concrete, time-bound human figures. The questing knight, the ancient *banais,* Dis, Persephone, Hades, the Sovereignty—all these mythic entities stand in tacit but powerful contrast to Dublin's (and history's) would-be mythic, which tends to be terminological merely. Phoenix Park, Chapelizod: whatever the derivation of the names (*Phoenix Park* is an ignorant mistranslation of the Gaelic placename), their implications have bled away into history, until with Chapelizod (Chapel of Iseult) even the mere term has eroded.

These extensions of the personal into the mythic and the psychic—hardly to be found in Kinsella's early work—ground the personal and the imaginative in something firmer than sentiment or desire by connecting them with culture, and they testify to the transcendent possibilities in phenomena, confirming the existence of the noumenal and its participation in phenomena. Most important, the transcendent possibilities reveal an escape from the perishability of the historical that entails no callow evasion of history.

Clearly manifest in all this is the primacy of pattern over person, as the poem proceeds from lower to higher and more comprehensive levels. As with all the conventional lyric phenomena in the poem, the poet-image itself is subsumed into noumenal pattern—which is to say that the bounded self of the early Kinsella dissolves into something rife with potentiality. Reviewing the development of the self he is presenting to Eleanor, he recalls an earlier self:

> A child stooped to the grass, picking and peeling
> And devouring mushrooms straight out of the ground:
> Death-pallor in their dry flesh, the taste of death
>
> (N, 76)

This figure metamorphoses into that figure of the daughter Sara in her "Communion finery" who both replicates and transforms her father's action, as we have seen. But both manifestations are taken up into pattern in the section of Part 2 devoted to *The dream.* In the "saturated depths" of "the ordeal cup,"[8] the figures are seen again, along with some others, in a progression in which person is an aspect of pattern:

---

8. This image is a carryover from the Prologue to *Wormwood,* but Kinsella has said that the cup in "Phoenix Park" is actually "a pint of stout" (O'Hara 1981, 10).

A child plucks death and tastes it; a shade watches
Over him; the child fades and the shade, made flesh,
Stumbles on understanding, begins to fade,

Bequeathing a child in turn; women-shapes pass
Unseeing, full of knowledge, through each other
. . . All gathered. And the crystal so increases,
Eliciting in its substance from the dark
The slowly forming laws it increases by.

(N, 78)

The vision of patterned change is the principal focus of this section of the poem. Phenomenal events like the glass of stout or the sight of their child plucking something from the grass tend to open into a kind of ontological revelation or, as the speaker makes clear with respect to Eleanor, lead the meditating consciousness to conceive a realm of the "Laws of order," the central property of the "crystal world," the ground of the phenomenal. His perception of pattern in those lines furnishes the meaning of that earlier manifestation years before in the rooms in Baggot Street, when

Attracted from the night by my wakefulness
Certain half-dissolved—half-formed—beings loomed close:
A child with eaten features eating something—
Another, with unfinished features, in white—
They hold hands. A shadow bends to protect them.

The shadow tries to speak, but its tongue stumbles.
A snake out of the void moves in my mouth, sucks
A triple darkness. . . .

(N, 84)

The poem here fades into conclusion—better, fades into possibility, since these last few lines will serve later as a prologue to the poems in Kinsella's next book, *Notes from the Land of the Dead*. What is taking place at this point is the gradual formation of a vision dependent neither on the happenstances of temporal actuality—history—nor the private vagaries of the "merely" personal, but on a conception of both categories as authentically rife with noumenal realities.

By this point as well the speaker has begun to comprehend the true meaning of his calling. The poem is diverted from what looks like a conventional opening:

                    we are leaving.
              You are quiet and watchful, this last visit.
              We pass the shapes of cattle blurred by moisture;
              A few deer lift up their wet horns from the grass
                                                        (*N*, 75)

a fair enough beginning for a seemingly conventional poem of departure,
but diverted by Eleanor's question into the investigative meditation I have
been describing. Acknowledging his abandonment of lyric, the speaker
proceeds through a stage of vague feelings of uncertainty and ignorance
and half-understood movements toward understanding.

The process is difficult to describe in an orderly way, because there is
a silent partner whose methods do not lend themselves to easy summary:
James Joyce, and specifically the Joyce of *Finnegans Wake*. He is openly
invoked in "Nightwalker," of course ("Joyce's Martello tower. . . .
Watcher in the tower, be with me now. . . . Turn your milky spectacles on
the sea . . . " *N*, 61) but as the H. C. Earwicker of the *Wake* he is also
playfully concealed: "Handclasp; I do not exist"; "Hesitant, cogitating,
exit" (*N*, 58, 65). In "Phoenix Park" he figures as an element in the
method. Like *Finnegans Wake*, the poem laminates whole clusters of issues
that seem distinct but turn out to be significantly isomorphic—the historical, the legendary, and the current, the personal, the familial, the political.
Polyvalent, palimpsest-like, yes—but the term *allegorical* cannot stretch
widely enough to cover the nature of poems like this. The events are
reminiscent of events in Wordsworth—a charged remembrance, a crisis of
the self, the compelling stranger whose presence springs a moral teaching:
events that have a place in a larger order of reality.

What looks like an all-too-conventional subordination of the feminine
in all this is similarly polyvalent. Eleanor is experienced throughout in a
fairly conventional imagery, as body—body clearly in contrast, as we have
seen, to the masculine poet as mind. But in one brief passage the poet
suddenly shares her imagery, when he "gives back" the laws of order he
has learned at her hands, "not as your body knows them. . . . But mental,
in my fever—mere idea." That is, the fever that began in "your body's
fever" as the poet stooped to kiss the ill Eleanor and then became the
"fever now that eats everything," finally, in a real step toward genuine
knowledge, is seen as characterizing the speaker himself. So in addition to
being a "preparation," as the poem entitles these lines, for *The dream* as
such, this is also preparation for the poet's progress beyond mere intellect
and beyond the gender conventions of lyric, preparation for his own
completion as a creative potentiality through the connection with Eleanor-

anima-hag-flesh-feminine. It is also the adumbration, as we shall see, of a whole new sense in Kinsella of how meanings are built.

The section from which these lines are quoted—the second—is the most relentlessly abstract in the poem, and the concluding phrase, "my fever—mere idea," is a true description of its orientation. That is why the resonance with such things as the symbolic marriage of king to Sovereignty is so important: it figures a potential depth in the male/mental poet's union with the female/fleshly, a union that from the male poet's standpoint constitutes the completion and enablement of the creative self. The rather thoroughgoing male orientation manifested here was soon to undergo extensive alteration in Kinsella's work. In "Phoenix Park" the feminine undergoes no transformation comparable to the poet's, and, *pace* his love for her, her most significant capability for him is to develop him; there is no curiosity about Eleanor's feelings about all this. In work to come, the axis of gender will dissolve under the poet's fascinating imagining of both the feminine and masculine principles. The poet's debt to the feminine, so to call it, will be paid in *Notes from the Land of the Dead*— where at the same time he will conduct the process of the completion of the creative self at a level considerably more profound. "Phoenix Park" initiates this process in taking up the lesson of "Traveller" and setting out to explore the poetic self by reaching far back into Irish tradition—beyond the threadbare stories Ireland tells itself about its recent history and the bitter allegories (Fox and Groom, for example) by which it expresses its sterile preoccupations with betrayal, beyond the iconic dead ends of the Easter Rising, the betrayal by the priests, and suchlike, into the far reaches of Irish prehistory. For the next decade and more, the problematic of the creative self will be Kinsella's point of departure for some of the most noteworthy poetry of our time.

3   Beyond Lyric
Notes from the Land of the Dead

The developments just described constitute more than thematic change: there is an additional significant operation going on in "Phoenix Park" that makes it a pivotal work. Kinsella begins there what will become a radical alteration in the handling of the significant entities in his poetry. Something approaching the outer limit of this alteration figured above, in the example from *Notes from the Land of the Dead* in the introductory chapter. It is among other things a move away from logic and from merely logical—that is, limited—language.

The wit in "Mirror in February" operates on the basis of defective analogy: pollarding a fruit tree seems to resemble shaving and is fruitful, whereas shaving is a downward-tending course of meaningless repetitions; but in the end the analogy proves less telling than the speaker at first fears, in that by grace of *grace* he transcends after all the limited possibilities available to trees. "Hacked clean for better bearing" is used as a figure of thought, and its happily inexact linking of humans and trees is based on logic, which the language here in no way strains; it handles meaning in a relatively straightforward way. So in "Traveller": though the associations of the owl are useful specifically to this poem—it is white, it flies, it is associated with divinity and wisdom—it is dealt with mainly as an owl *tout simple*. At bottom even the language in "Museum" operates logically. Its analytic moves simply uncover the logical implications of museumdom. The institution is basically an exemplum; the language in which it is considered is figurative in a way that presumably brings out certain hidden or heretofore not-thought-of aspects of such institutions—it "squats closer on its hoard," and its stones "are speechless with fatigue." The middle stanza comes close to a kind of linguistic deconstruction of

61

the conventional conception of museum ("webs of corridors / . . . Catch the onward turbulence of forms / . . . flux disperses / In order everywhere"), and in the light of this operation the poem does seem a step beyond the strategies of "Mirror in February"—but only a step.

For the museum remains a museum, as the owl remains an owl and the trees trees. They are the given of each poem. The given in "Phoenix Park," on the other hand, tends either to be dissolved into its mythic or psychic relationships or to be turned aside as the empty matter of lyric. The opening stanzas of the fourth part make the latter move perfectly clear: they tick off one by one the lyric clichés offered by Dublin-in-history:

> The tires are singing, cornering back and forth
> In our green world again; into groves of trees,
> By lake and open park, past the hospital
> . . . .
> An eighteenth century prospect to the sea—
> River haze; gulls; spires glitter in the distance
> Above faint multitudes
>
> (N, 82)

And all this is immediately sent packing:

> Dublin, the umpteenth city of confusion . . .
> A theatre for the quick articulate,
> The agonized genteel, their artful watchers . . .
> Malice as entertainment. Asinine feast
> Of sowthistles and brambles! And there dead men,
> Half hindered by dead men, tear down dead beauty.

Having left the Park in part 2, poet and wife have presumably left its underworld for Dublin's upperworld, but upperworld Dublin proves in these lines to be a worse-than-sterile necropolis. Turning from entities like these, which are seen as totally external, the poet and Eleanor are to "Return by the mental ways we have ourselves / Established"—which sounds at first like a simple inner opposed to a simple outer. But the "ways" are "visages of memory / Set at every turn: where we smiled . . . or stood . . . where we roamed," which is to say external but rendered meaningful by their participation in the experience of speaker and beloved —inner and outer conjoined.

Kinsella is leaving behind the strategy of invoking, by naming, entities whose meanings in a simple sense are familiar and given (owl, lake, lover), and which are then poetically exploited. In "Phoenix Park" he is moving toward a strategy whereby meaning is something gradually accumulated. The at first highly abstract notion of *tissue,* for example, in "Phoenix Park" —"the tissues of order" that "Form under your stare"—is even more abstract in the passage about the "total hunger," the ghostly form that "Gropes out . . . / Eating new tissue down into existence." But it gains definition partly by virtue of the relations it enters into and partly by its participation in more concrete contexts. Facing the possibility that the lovers might evade or reject the ordeal the facing of which might enable them to grow, and warning that

> Then the vivifying eye clouds, and the thin
> Mathematic tissues loosen, and the cup
> Thickens, and order dulls and dies
> (*N,* 81)

—the poem knits the concept *tissue* to the morality of the lovers' struggle for persistence and growth. When the concept joins their life of concrete sexuality ("My past alive in you, a gift of tissue / Torn free from my life in an odour of books") it is to place that sexuality also as an active participant on the spectrum of moral significances the image has been accruing since its first use in the poem, while the sexuality helps establish the fuller meaning of the abstract metaphor with which the poet began. By similar proceeding, the metaphysical base of the ordeal the lovers must face, and paradoxically welcome, comes gradually to be figured in the image of the crystal, the eerily abstract manifestation of the noumenal underpinning of humane consciousness that is ultimately concretized—domesticated—in the poet's recall of the scene in his rooms, another time, another place, a place perhaps sheltered and private, like a poem:

> where naked by firelight
> We stood and rested from each other and took
> Our burden from the future, eyes crystalline.
> (*N,* 83)

For the Kinsella of these lines, then, words are becoming something other than known or preestablished entities referring to other known entities that happen to engage his attention. If meanings can be built or gradually assembled by the interaction of experience with the repetition, cross-reference, and recurrence of words, then the nature of language has become something deeper than what Kinsella was apparently willing to claim in his earlier writing. Though his own comments on the poems in this volume seemed to restrict language, as we have seen (p. 36), to structure-

building or the rendering of theme, even the language of, say, "Ballydavid
Pier," a less ambitious poem than these last three, presents a mode of
description pressed intensely toward metaphor:

> —A swollen blind brow
> Humbly crumpled over
> Budding limbs, unshaken
> By the spasms of birth or death.
> . . . .
> The misbirth touches the surface
> And glistens like quicksilver.
>
> (N, 7)

Both of these developments in *Nightwalker* bespeak a changed conception of the powers of mind and the powers of language. Kinsella has come
a long way from his lament in 1962 that an Irish poet can deploy only a
fragile or limited sense of identity and from his conviction that poetry
must hope for no more than stemming the tide. A vivifying sense of the
unity of existence informs Kinsella's use of those lines in "Phoenix Park,"
and many culminations. The solitary male of "Baggot Street Deserta,"
entirely given over to words, has become part of a creative sexual pair; the
naïve and fragmented intellect has been united with flesh; time, that hope-
less medium of entropy, has fused with space. Language is finally understood as profoundly rooted in the human phenomena of which it is both
formulation and organic part—and above it all, phenomena have found
the fostering bed of the noumenal.

The three poems, "Nightwalker," "Ritual of Departure," and "Phoenix Park," that conclude *Nightwalker* describe a clear trajectory from the
revelation of the aimless fragmentation, moral emptiness, and life-threat-
ening mutability of the historical to the successful completion of a quest
for redemptive forms of life not isolated from noumenal foundations. The
mind behind these poems has realized the completion of a creative self; it
has in some sense at least glimpsed the noumenal principles by which that
completion is attained and by which it must be sustained if it is to be
sustained at all; and Kinsella has made important steps toward the development of a poetic language that can transcend conventional lyric and
move toward the larger goals he is already sensing. No longer responding
lyrically to "situations," he is about to undertake a pursuit of the Real.

That pursuit could not be carried on at any interesting level within the
limits set either by his own earlier lyric practices or those of the conven-

tional lyric in general—that all-purpose congeries of poetic forms. The "level" at which his next collection, *Notes from the Land of the Dead*, showed him to be operating was such that without poems like "Phoenix Park" as a middle term, the work would seem poetry from another planet, compared to *Another September*. For one thing, it is a composed *book*, after the manner or method of the later Yeats. Kinsella had obviously been attracted by this possibility as early as *Downstream*. *Another September* had printed its poems one after the other, and though interrelations might be found, the table of contents seems essentially a list. But James Liddy's review of the 1961 *Poems and Translations* noted that Kinsella had rearranged there some of the poems from *Another September* and had sectioned the poems into four specific mood-groups. *Downstream*, he added, arranged the earlier poems differently still and organized a middle section around the long poems "A Country Walk," "Old Harry," and "Downstream"(Liddy 1962). But in *Notes from the Land of the Dead* we confront a principle more radical still. Almost none of its poems stands fully by itself; each interacts with others in the book to such an extent that no single poem can be fully appprehended without reference to the entire collection.

Its separate sections, *"an egg of being," "a single drop,"* and *"nightnothing,"* reach no novelistic "conclusion," but the last poem in the collection belongs absolutely where it is, helping as it does to place the other poems in one's experience of the whole book. For Kinsella this method is intensely meant. Years after the publication of *Notes from the Land of the Dead* he said to John Haffenden, "Hopefully, my poems are fitting into a larger whole in which they'll have larger and more organically related meanings. . . . Some of the poems that I'm most committed to are in *Notes from the Land of the Dead*...and those are completely exploratory still." "Tear," he added, is a poem "that doesn't close and still has the potentiality for development" (Haffenden 1981, 104–105). These comments, like the seemingly unexceptionable remark to Haffenden that "At a certain stage I found myself writing a book of poems rather than merely collecting poems into a book," point to the very redefinition of the boundaries of poems.

"Phoenix Park" itself presses toward the redefinition of a whole range of practices and categories, including "the Real" itself. Like the earlier "Baggot Street Deserta," it is partly about the artistic act (one of the recurring subjects in Kinsella's earlier work), but unlike that poem it strives to link the implications of the act of poetizing with further concerns —this is the position Kinsella had adumbrated in the 1962 interview with Peter Orr:

My earliest poems were about the artistic act and I still do them, but they are becoming slightly more elaborate and in a peculiar way the idea of artistic creation and the idea of the passing of time are becoming fused together. I have not yet written a poem in which this process is embodied. (Orr 1966, 105)

"Phoenix Park" clearly (perhaps even painfully) aims at being a poem in which that process is embodied, and one of the poems in the earlier pages of *Nightwalker,* "Soft Toy," suggests what might be involved when the line of development laid down there is decisively pursued. Clearly an allegory on the artistic act, it is about the nature of poems and their reception ("My face of beaten fur / Responds as you please: if you do not smile / It does not smile . . ."), and possibly about lovers and spouses in its awareness that persons are in some large part functions of other persons' responses—an idea that has considerable bearing on the nature of Kinsella's work at this point. But it is certainly an image of the relation between the poet's processes and an audience:

> I lie limp with use and re-use, listening.
> Loose ends of conversations, hesitations,
> Half-beginnings that peter out in my presence,
> Are enough. I understand, with a flame of shame
> Or a click of ease or joy, inert. Knowledge
> Into resignation: the process drives deeper,
> Grows clearer, eradicating chance growths of desire
> —And colder: all possibilities of desire.
>
> My button-brown hard eyes fix on your need
> To grow, as you crush me with tears and throw me aside.
> Most they reflect, but something absorb. . . .
> . . . .
> I face the dark with eyes that cannot close
> —The cold, outermost points of your will, as you sleep.
> Between your tyrannous pressure and the black
> Resistance of the void my blankness hardens
> To a blunt probe, a cold pitted grey face.
>
> (*N,* 47–48)

These are the words of a Joycean/Kinsellan poet levitating above events, as the early Kinsella felt that a poet must (Orr 1966, 106)—in this case not particularly liking it. But to face the dark with eyes that cannot close is a job not only for poets but for any seriously functioning mind confronting, say, history—or situated between a tyrannical deity and the ethical blank of mortal existence. The poem is an example of the poet's developing awareness that the poetic act opens out conceptually into the ambience of other intelligential acts, that the problems of the poetic mind are simply problems of mind.

"The Route of the Táin" and "Worker in Mirror, at His Bench," from "Other Poems" in *Notes from the Land of the Dead and Other Poems,* are continuous with this aspect of "Soft Toy," with the difference that they focus on achievements, and the tone of ironic bafflement is left behind. Taken together, in fact, the poems manifest an increasing degree of openness of self and scene to each other. In "Soft Toy" the integrity of both scene and speaking self is to a degree ambiguous; in "The Route of the Táin" the scene opens to the self, while in "Worker in Mirror, at His Bench" the self opens (the term is too limited) to scene. Involved in an excursion attempting to follow the route of the army of Mebh in its raid on Coole, the poet and his friends in "The Route of the Táin" find themselves hopelessly astray:

> Scattering in irritation . . . who had set out
> so cheerfully to celebrate our book;
> cheerfully as we made and remade it
> through a waste of hours, content to "enrich the present
> honouring the past," each to his own just function . . .
> Wandering off, ill-sorted,
> like any beasts of the field,
> One snout honking disconsolate,
> another burrowing in its pleasures
>
> (*NLD*, 53–54)

An unsought blessing from the natural world in the form of a red fox dashing across the landscape draws the poet's attention to the proper landmarks, and the impasse is breached, in one of those revelations of useful order the early Kinsella was rarely allowed:

> For a heartbeat, in alien certainty,
> we exchanged looks. We should have known it, by now:
> the process, the whole tedious
> enabling ritual! Flux brought to fullness
> —saturated—the clouding over—dissatisfaction
> spreading slowly like an ache: something
> reduced shivering suddenly into meaning
> along new boundaries.
>
> (*NLD*, 54)

This is not how the early Kinsella read landscape, this flowing of landscape into mind.

"Worker in Mirror" is a more complicated utterance with similar implications. Moved to a deeper consideration of the significance of his art by intensely ironic exchanges with some visitors to his workshop, the Worker "bends closer, testing the work":

> The bright assembly begins to turn in silence.
> The answering brain glitters—one system
> answering another. The senses enter
> and reach out with a pulse of pleasure
> to the four corners of their own wilderness.
>
> (*NLD*, 58)

As his naïve attempts in the first part of the poem to "understand" the work recede into the background, the worker in mirror visualizes a sequence of possible referents: a succession of masks or heads, of gold, of silver, bronze, and iron. The contemplation (or conceit; it is hard to tell which) conducts his mind to a frightening vision of light "hammered / into two blazing eyes; / all the darkness / into one wolf-muzzle":

> Resist!
> An unholy tongue laps, tastes
> brothers' thick blood.
> Forget!
>
> (*NLD*, 59)

The whole vision is the artist's projection of himself into the work and his being at first seduced by "a false infinity," as Kinsella has explained (O'Hara 1981, 13), into a delusive conception of a Golden Age self which degenerates as the vision continues. The end point is the frightening vision of the partial truth of the wolf-muzzle, the revelation of the savagery that has lain at the core of the human psyche since the days of Cain and beyond. The meditation closes with a vision strikingly similar to some of "Soft Toy":

> a marble carcase
> where no living thing can have crept,
> below the last darkness,
> slowly, as the earth ages,
> blurring with pressure.
> The calm smile of a half-

buried face: eyeball
blank, the stare inward
to the four corners of
what foul continuum . . .

(*NLD*, 59)

Kinsella's commentary on these lines, "The act of understanding initiated by the worker, as observer, when he looks into the construct, ends in an understanding of what lies in wait for unreasonable hope" (O'Hara 1981, 14), sounds like a return to the beleaguered stoicism of the early Kinsella, but the enlarged scope of the poem as well as its more ambitious strategy mark it as a clear advance. The enlarged scope is embedded in the poem's resonances: the ancient theory of Ages, the echoes of Belshazzar's Feast,[1] the glimpse of Irish history in the allusion to Ferdia's death at the hands of Cuchulain, even the urge to repress and to flee, rather than stoically to face, evil—all of these argue the embeddedness of the moment in a time flow conceived of as organic and continuous with the psychic depths of the artist himself.

The speaker's fantasies recall the expansion of the self evinced by "Phoenix Park" and link up with the profoundly exploratory concerns that direct all of *Notes from the Land of the Dead*—an exploration that will extend from the grounds of the self to the nature of the real. Thus "Soft Toy" is a conscious mind's considering, with conscious wit, the implications of a situation, implications like those of "Mirror in February" and its fellows: for all their emotional weight, they are essentially logical. But the language and the visions in "Worker in Mirror, At His Bench" go beyond both logic and conscious wit. The consolatory dream of the marble torso with "eyeball blank" comes only after the frightening earlier vision of the bloody wolf-muzzle, itself the sardonic, apocalyptic end point of the worker's musing on the Golden Age, and of it all, only the Golden Age fantasy is rooted in conscious rationality. The important issues come from below, from "below," moreover, in a self whose boundaries are more ambiguous than anything the earlier Kinsella seemed likely to entertain, and this is a central characteristic of Kinsella's work in and after *Notes from the Land of the Dead*.

This ambitious meditation on the poetic act is radically different from

---

1. Daniel 5:4, 5:22 and 5:23: "They drank wine, and praised the gods of gold, and of silver, of brass, of iron, of wood, and of stone. . . . thou . . . , O Belshazzar, hast not humbled thine heart. . . . thou hast praised the gods of silver, and gold, of brass, iron, wood, and stone, which see not, nor hear, nor know."

those earlier efforts—"Baggot Street Deserta," for example—in the relationship it posits between the creative self and its creative behavior. "Baggot Street Deserta" presents a speaker—what W. J. McCormack has characterized as "the transparent, autonomous consciousness" that narrated Kinsella's earlier poems (McCormack 1987, 69)—meditating his calling as he might consider a natural object, as something in which he of course has a stake but which is fundamentally external to himself—in the sense that a job of work is external to the workman, however deep his or her commitment to it. Not so with "Worker in Mirror." Beginning at least with "Phoenix Park," Kinsella carries out a persistent relaxation of the boundedness that had characterized his early writing, and the conventional boundary between scene and spectator, concept and thinker, begins dramatically to dissolve. It is at this point especially that he begins to use the disconcerting shifts in point of view, the sudden dissolutions of scene or event into mysterious analogues, and the dissolution of the very limits of the poem that have become so characteristic of his poetry.

What is manifested in these last three poems is a multifaceted revision of the very concept of lyric akin to what Donald Davie ascribes to Czeslaw Milosz (Davie 1986).[2] Davie's argument begins with the position that in the conventional lyric a stable or unified speaker—McCormack's "transparent, autonomous consciousness"—"occupies a fixed point in a landscape, and the assertions that he makes are to be understood as true only in relation to that fixed point, in the context of a special occasion and a mood which that occasion provokes" (Davie 1986, 4). Milosz steps outside these conventions; his implied speakers have no such stable identity and occupy no fixed point either spatial or temporal, and in much of his work he quite wipes out the specifications of scene and occasion that typify lyrics such as Gray's "Elegy" or Wordsworth's "Tintern Abbey"— or the Greater Romantic Ode in general, it would seem (Davie 1986, 48). Whatever one's assessment of these characterizations of the conventional lyric, what Davie ascribes to Milosz here is almost exactly what Kinsella does in the work after *Nightwalker*.

The bravura style confining the poetic experience to a field of purely aesthetic action, the distant regard conceded to history and locale, the

2. In a different version of my argument here, McCormack (68–69) points to Kinsella's *New Poems* of 1973 as the first work to display "Kinsella's growing interest in writing a poetry which spreads outwards beyond the conventional structures of the self-like stanza, the psyche-identical poem. . . . The transparent, autonomous consciousness" to which I refer above "is giving way to more fluid psychological structures which might even be driven to extend to [or?] replace the disintegrating *Gesellschaft* which is the state today."

bounded mind restricted to observation and response, the ontological tidiness in the interview with Peter Orr in 1962, with its talk of the poet's obligation to "levitate above the circumstances" and its attempt to compartmentalize Kinsella's poetizing from his Catholicism and his Irishness—none of this could withstand the turn of mind underlying poems like these last three. What was prepared in "Phoenix Park" and affirmed here was a liberation from any and all kinds of compartmental thinking, including the sense that language owes its primary allegiance to the claims of the putatively actual. Whereas Kinsella's earlier work, for all its unquestioned virtuosity, rarely calls into question the referential adequacy of language or the integrity of exterior fact, the kind of verse signaled by "Phoenix Park" builds a language and a reality from the inside out.

These poems manifest, then, Kinsella's developing new sense of what we can call, after Davie, the insufficiency of lyric. More specifically, it involved three major developments: a changed sense of how human reality is constituted, coordinate with a changed sense of the legitimate powers of both language and the imagination, and a changed sense of the poetic self. Formally or structurally, what was involved was a new way of using figurative language, abrupt alterations in point of view, a frequent overriding of conventions of both time and space, and a far less firmly contained speaker or narrator than Kinsella had employed earlier.

Late in "Phoenix Park" the speaker muses on a thought he had at the time of "Baggot Street Deserta":

> A thought of fires in the hearts of darknesses,
> A darkness at the heart of every fire,
> Darkness, fire, darkness, threaded on each other—
>
> The orders of stars fixed in abstract darkness,
> Darknesses of worlds sheltering in their light;
> World darkness harbouring orders of cities
> Whose light at midnight harbours human darkness;
> The human dark pierced by solitary fires.
>
> (N, 83)

These lines, which record a moment when "Loneliness drew into order," acknowledging the dark side of every joy, also have to do with how things take on value and meaning. Darkness here is a necessary condition of light, as light of dark. Each shelters its opposite other, so that it is no longer meaningful to ascribe positive value exclusively to either, and opposites stand in a relation of *enabling* opposition. The very name of the park and title of the poem of course underscore this: destructive fire is a necessary condition of the rebirth of the phoenix, and Phoenix Park itself, historically nul site of a useless political murder (its very name an etymological mistake), becomes the locale of the poet's psychic rebirth; negation is a necessary condition of affirmation. Such "facts" are not merely subjective but ontologically firm, grounded in part, as we shall see, in theories of C. G. Jung that make claims about both psychic experience and the nature of reality; the assertions in the verse, accordingly, are not merely figurative. The poetry after "Phoenix Park" does in fact treat meaning— linguistic, conceptual, and experiential—as a different phenomenon from what it was in the early work, and it becomes impossible to discuss Kinsella's sense of reality separately from his sense of the nature and powers of language.

For example, well into *Notes from the Land of the Dead,* a poem called "At the Crossroads" presents a revision of the owl in "Traveller":

> A white ghost flickered into being
> and disappeared near the tree tops.
> An owl in silent scrutiny
> with blackness in her heart. She
> who succeeds from afar . . .
> > The choice—
> the drop with deadened wing-beats; some creature
> torn and swallowed; her brain, afterward,
> staring among the rafters in the dark
> until hunger returns.
>
> > > (*NLD*, 35)

This female owl is a particular manifestation of a principle meditated in the stanza preceding:

> . . . all mouths everywhere so
> in their need, turning on each furious
> other. Flux of forms
> in a great stomach: living meat torn off,
> enduring in one mess of terror
> every pang it sent through every thing
> it ever, in shudders of pleasure, tore.

As an anthology piece the poem is a commentary on fundamentals; it presents a glimpse into the darkness in which we inevitably, if only sometimes, move. The beast that tears knows and itself endures the terror it deals out, and, not unlike a predatory poet in the phenomenal world, it possesses a brain that stares in the dark. But the poem does not have its full meaning by itself; its images and concepts participate in a network of developing meanings, informed by versions of its images in poems preceding and following it, and on the other hand affecting the significance of those poems by being what it is itself. The imagery of this specific predatory act is explored elsewhere in the book almost element by element.

The opening lines of "A Hand of Solo" could, though they do not, present the actions of a predator:

> Lips and tongue
> wrestle the delicious
> life out of you
> (*NLD*, 13)

The scene happens to be the conclusion of lovemaking, (or an infant at the breast, according to Kinsella), but the speaker's thoughts are awakened to another occasion on which lips and tongue extracted "delicious life": biting into that pomegranate his grandmother had given him (above, p. 11), he sank his teeth into it,

> loosening the packed mass of dryish beads
> from their indigo darkness.
> I drove my tongue among them
>
> and took a mouthful, and slowly
> bolted them. My throat filled
> with a rank, Arab bloodstain.
> (*NLD*, 15)

This passage lends a retrospective coloration to the imagery that describes the lovemaking, and it would not be too much to say that the correlation with lovemaking lends a (superficially bizarre) coloration to the predatory action of the owl and the eating of the fruit by the boy. Predation becomes simple enraged savagery in "Ely Place," where the poet-speaker fantasizes a gruesome attack on a young woman passing by:

> A blood vision
> started out of the brick; the box
> of keys in my pocket—I am opening it,
> tongue-tied. I unpick the little
> pen-knife and dig it in her throat,
> her spirting gullet!
>
> (*NLD*, 44)

a savage revision of the loving lines at the opening of "A Hand of Solo,"
asserting the demonic underside of sexual arousal. What is gradually being
built up is a resonating set of interrelated feelings or concepts: predation-
nourishment-sexual love, loveplay-attack-eating; sexual thrusting-stab-
bing-biting.

In what is at once a matter of language and a matter of concepts
extending to implicit assertions about reality, the value of the imagery of
darkness in the poems, ambiguous in itself, is similarly tied to participation with other imageries: the "indigo darkness" offered by the pomegranate seeds is both a locale of nourishment and, in connection with the
"rank, Arab bloodstain," linked to slaughter. Darkness surrounds the central human figure of the collection, what Kinsella has referred to as "the
all-swallowing hag," but which is often manifested as the poet's possibly
loving but certainly forbidding and mysterious grandmother. She is invariably dressed in black, and her customary locale is the setting of the pomegranate experience, the dark shop backed by a gloomy scullery into which
from time to time she vanishes. These dark enclosures are as inscrutable as
"Her stale abyss," of which the poet thinks when she hugs him to her lap
(*NLD*, 15), and they contribute to his sense of her as unfathomable and
threatening. The emotional bearing, ultimately the meaning, of these enclosures is in turn related to things like the "Flux of forms in a great
stomach" in "At the Crossroads" and the cave in another poem, "Survivor." There a figure who fuses the mythical personages Fintan and Tuan
mac Carell, lone survivors of early stages in the "taking" of Ireland, sprawls
in his cavern, where he hears "far back, a lost echoing / single drop: / the
musk of glands and bloody gates and alleys" (*NLD*, 30). Such lines color
and are colored by the experiences at the grandmother's deathbed in
"Tear." Sent into her room to pay his last respects, the poet recalls
thinking,

> Was I to kiss her? As soon
> kiss the damp that crept
> in the flowered walls
> of this pit.
>
> (*NLD*, 21)

Room, pit, cavern, stomach, scullery, pomegranate, mouth—these enclosures (which are also openings) take on various meanings, and they have to be read in connection with the further motif of entering or enterings. The boy's entering into his dying grandmother's room in "Tear" is futile; not only can he not bring himself to kiss her, he clearly cannot assimilate her. Here as in all the poems she figures in, she is left moot, unplaced, a figure coterminous with her acts and speeches because her chronicler could not master the feelings or language to explain her; enough that he can recount the events.

In "Survivor" a failed communal entering into a new land has shriveled into Fintan/Tuan's retreat into his sheltering and confining cavern, and his story is a saga shriveled into a personal narrative of perplexing loss. Like the boy, he can recite events, both promising ("we came in sight of promontories beautiful beyond description") and disastrous ("Everyone falling sick, after a time"), but that is as far as comprehension goes, and the poem trails off in an image of the speaker's own inability to register meaning:

> I must remember
> and be able some time to explain.
>
> .
>
> There is nothing here for sustenance.
> Unbroken sleep were best.
> Hair. Claws. Grey.
> Naked. Wretch. Wither.[3]
>
> (*NLD*, 33)

The poet himself had an experience related to this, recounted in the anecdote of a local landmark, the Robbers' Den, in "The High Road." He recalls his daring boyish invasion of this romantically named place:

> I crept up
> the last stretch to the big hole
> full of fright, once, and knelt
> on the clay to look inside:
> it was only a hollow someone made,
> with a dusty piece of man's dung

3. The final three lines here conflate lines from the chants of Fintan ("Unbroken sleep were best") and Tuan ("Hair. Claws. Grey. / Naked. Wretched. Wither"). Fintan's line is the translation of R. A. S. Macalister (Macalister 1939, 211). Tuan's is from R. I. Best's translation of de Jubainville's account of the Partholonian invasion (Arbois de Jubainville 1903, 29).

and a few papers in a corner,
and bluebottles.

(*NLD*, 17)

The promised joys of sensational exotica fizzle into trivia, thus echoing if
not quite recapitulating the fate of Tuan/Fintan, and the implications
range from the casually ironic to the political and sexual. Add the concept
of entering, then, to the list of ideas and images which are seen in these
poems to assemble meaning as the collection unfolds.

In such passages the boundaries of conventional lyric practice are
clearly dissolved. In connection with what he said to Haffenden about
composing books rather than separate poems, Kinsella added, "I hope the
echoes of one poem or sequence go on and get caught by the next. The
poems I'm working on now will, I hope, gather up previous work as well
as move forward" (Haffenden 1981, 105). And as with heretofore separate poems, so, obviously, with meaning. In this poetry the designatable
comprises not a collection of reference points in a clear reality but a
congeries of resonant events, dynamic nodes in an interplay of emotional
energies, involving a gradual accretion of meaning such that at book's end
a given manifestation of any one is instinct with the experiential significance of all the others.

By the same token, the language in which experiences here are presented is not the ostensive language of the early work, words whose
meanings are largely given and whose function is adequately to describe
clear facts, but a more constitutive language, tied far more intimately to
the phenomenological status of the dubious objects to which it seems to
refer. Such remarks are one way of describing symbolism, and when we
add the dynamic interplay of opposites in that passage from "Phoenix
Park" an inevitable resonance with W. B. Yeats suggests itself. But
Kinsella's conceptions here are not cyclical or sequential as Yeats's are; the
more pertinent correlative is the thought of Jung, whose speculative visions (and whose skepticism of conventional psychic boundaries) lay just
on the horizon at the point of Kinsella's work represented in "Phoenix
Park." The distinction is important, for he is not moving toward a theory
of history as Yeats ultimately was, but toward a theory of knowledge and
morale.[4]

---

4. The most compendious study of Kinsella's use of Jung is Carolyn Rosenberg's
doctoral dissertation mentioned earlier. Rosenberg (1980) was the first commentator to take
Kinsella's Jungian bent as seriously as his work requires, but Johnston's discussion (1987) is
a more penetrating elucidation.

1. The Robbers' Den. "It was only a hollow someone made, / with a dusty piece of man's dung . . . and bluebottles."

It was around the time some of the poems in *Nightwalker and Other Poems* were gestating, in fact, that Kinsella took up Jolande Jacobi's exposition of the theories of C. G. Jung (Jacobi 1951); the implications of poems like "Soft Toy" and "Worker in Mirror" suggest why this event was to have such a profound impact on the poetry. The terms in which Kinsella himself has spoken of Jung clearly connect with his already developing move away from the boundedness of his early poetics:

> Jung helped me to my present understanding of what [the poetic process] is: the process whereby . . . experience is ingested, processed, deposited, prepared for use, made ready. . . . That's the interior process. The process of writing itself is analogous. It begins with the realization that important connections have suddenly been made, enabling a whole matrix to emerge from the subconscious. You are then in position more or less like that of a miner: you're in the dark but you have a direction and you can start working toward something. (O'Hara 1981, 8)

The poet's feelings on confronting Jung must have been like Ezra Pound's when he opened the manuscripts of Ernest Fenellosa or Eliot's when he first read F. H. Bradley. But the terms of Kinsella's praise of Jung here need to be noted. Not beguiled merely by the Jungian *concepts* that can be so seductive for certain kinds of literary critic—collective unconscious, anima, and the like—he is clearly speaking of Jung as a *structural* and *methodological* model. It is in this sense that the poetry at least from *Notes from the Land of the Dead* on manifests a pervasive interpenetration of Kinsellan and Jungian ways of thinking. The unfolding or elaborating meanings in the foregoing poems, for example, manifest an expressive version of *amplification,* the specifically Jungian method of reading dreams. According to Jung, the order in which dreams occur "does not always coincide with the actual inner order of meaning. . . . For the real arrangement of dreams is a *radial* one; it is grouped around a 'center of significance' " (Jacobi 1951, 98), and this is an apt image of how the issues in *Notes from the Land of the Dead* are uttered. As elaborated by Jolande Jacobi, amplification is

> a broadening and enrichment of the dream content with all possible similar, analogous images. It is . . . distinguished from free association in that the associations are contributed not only by the patient or dreamer but also by the physician. . . . However various these images may be, they must nevertheless all stand in a meaningful, more or less close relation to the dream content that is to be interpreted. . . . amplification is accordingly a kind of limited, bound, and directed association that re-

turns ever and again to the center of significance given in the dream. (Jacobi 1951, 109)

Thus the feminine in Kinsella's later work becomes the totality of everything—desirable, frightening, passive, resented, active, nurturing—the psyche has experienced, felt, or been led to feel or know about femaleness. The poems do not articulate its "meaning," or the "meaning" of love or of savagery or of "How I felt about Granny." They furnish the *ground* of meaning, the total zone of feeling from which radiate the speaker's conscious-world conceptions. In the structure Kinsella is elaborating in these poems, nothing "means" much by itself, and we are invited to read poems as we read experience: not in terms of representation, as an array of symbols or of things neatly designated, but as an unfolding series of phenomena always cognitively interrelated. In short, the conception of signification the foregoing pages have been ascribing to *Notes from the Land of the Dead* constitutes more than a mere strategy of presentation; it amounts to a theory of meaning, and it is part of the large development that gave Kinsella's journalistic critics such grief and his later poetry such profundity.

The third central development in Kinsella's revision of the conventional lyric in the work after *Nightwalker* was his vigorously renovated sense of the self. The not wholly jesting description of his early poetic stance as "the blank stare, the noting down of the event," with its hint of more or less desperate disdain (Orr 1966, 106), truly bespoke the boundedness of the self that limited the power of Kinsella's early bravura performances. We have seen that boundedness breaking down, or being rejected, in the poetry in *Nightwalker,* and some years later, in the interview with John Haffenden, Kinsella regretted the limitations, as he saw it, of even that work. Addressing a question about "sarcasm" in "Nightwalker," he said,

> Those were easy targets. [Now] I would step back and let the opinions of the main character emerge without feeling committed to them as a writer, even though he is of course oneself. The creative response separates itself even [as] to the actual protagonist, who happens to be oneself; another aspect of the consciousness deals in the creative understanding of this self who is dramatically captured. (Haffenden 1981, 106)

Such distance toward the protagonist looks like a reversion to the boundedness of the early work, but what Kinsella is actually describing is the same breaking up of the stable lyric self that Davie and McCormack describe. The conception at the center of *Notes from the Land of the Dead* and the poetry that followed is of a self in varying degrees continuous with what it is beholding, or somehow constituted by whatever process it finds itself in—in marked contrast to the conventional lyric self that observes, reflects upon, but easily can (or sadly must) withdraw from the exterior scenes before which it is placed.

For one thing, the narrator of many of the poems in *Notes from the Land of the Dead* seems to evade location in time; normal temporality seems irrelevant to the the operations of consciousness. "Hand of Solo" looks at first like a poem of reminiscence, with the narrator thinking back to some experiences of his childhood. But it begins in the present and in the present tense, and after those lines not recording but expressing the afterglow of lovemaking there occurs a casual-seeming dissolution of time in the third stanza, casually disguised, as it seems, by the syntax, which leaves speaker and audience immersed in both the "present" moment and the time of the childhood scene that is both past and, in terms of the poem, still to come:

> In the firelight glow
> the flickering
>   shadows softly
> come and go up on the shelf:
> red heart and black spade
>   hid in the kitchen dark.
>   (*NLD*, 23)

The abrupt shift into the past tense and the reference to playing cards occur because by means of a strategy that may owe something to the methods of the Nighttown episode in *Ulysses* the present scene has faded into the incident from the past and the speaker is no longer talking of himself as an adult but as a child.[5] The rest of the poem is without any semblance of *commentary* by the speaker; all is presented in the matter-of-fact, uncomprehending language of the boy he is remembering himself as. In short, the voice of the poem is less a genuine speaker than something

---

5. The contrast here with the handling of shifts of time in traditional lyrics is perhaps too obvious for comment. But Kinsella's technique would seem to be another aspect of the legacy of Joyce, whose handling of time shifts in the Nighttown episode evoked counterparts in *The Wasteland,* among other modernist works. In any case, Kinsella's adaptation of this originally novelistic procedure is obviously part of his movement beyond the limits of conventional lyric.

that has to be described almost only as the-presence-of-a-consciousness, and the identity of the self that begins the poem is as fluid as his command of the scene in which he finds himself —or the scene's command of him. In a way the speaker of the poems that follow (a child; the poet-adult does not return during this section of the book) is considerably less empowered than I seem to have been attempting to claim; but the point just *is* the fluidity of a lyric self immersed in an utterly nonlinear pool of time. Embedded in, rather than witnessing, the experience presented, the speaking self seems actually to be part of a flood of metamorphosis. In Jungian terms, he (or it) has given up egopower to achieve a truer identity.

At the end of "Tear" the dissolution is focused more directly, if more subtly, on the speaking self. The child kneels at his grandmother's deathbed and sinks his face "in the chill / and smell of her black aprons," whereupon

> Snuff and musk, the folds against my eyelids,
> carried me into a derelict place
> smelling of ash: unseen walls and roofs
> rustle like breathing.
>
> I found myself disturbing
> dead ashes for any trace
> of warmth, when far off
> in the vaults a single drop
>
> splashed.
>
> (*NLD*, 21)

His speech, that is, has become what will be the discourse of Fintan in "Survivor," four poems later in the book—Fintan who lurks, in anguished despair, in his cave, where

> Far back, a lost echoing
> single drop:
> the musk of glands
> and bloody gates and alleys.
> (*NLD*, 30)

Though readers won't know it until they come upon the later poem, the narrating identity of "Tear" has become continuous with the narrating identity of "Survivor." Unlike the self of the early collections, which was taken for granted in the way usual with selves, this one is embarked upon an account of its own genesis. It is not really until the subsequent collection, *Peppercanister Poems 1972–1978,* that we again encounter in Kinsella's work the more nearly conventional poetry of public address.

It is, of course, both artificial and to some extent trivializing to separate the three issues of self, language, and meaning. Once Kinsella moves away from the conventional or traditional lyric self and moves beyond the stance toward language in the conventional lyric, each of the triad of issues I have been tracing becomes a function of the others. As in Joyce (even something as early as *A Portrait of the Artist as a Young Man*), self and language seem extensions of one another. But since the name of Joyce has come up again, it might be important to remark here on what Kinsella is *not* doing in such lines. He is not doing what Patrick Kavanaugh seems to have thought Joyce did. Scorning large public issues himself, Kavanaugh asserted that "The things that matter are casual, insignificant little things," and of Joyce he added that he "is interested in the mind of the man who has put five shillings on a horse. Joyce . . . shows that in the end these private lives are the only lives that matter."[6]

Joyce is indeed a force in Kinsella's work at this point, but Kinsella saw him rather as laying hold on little things as embodiments of big things,[7] and his own following of that practice is part of what sets him apart from most of his contemporaries. To instance, for example, as some have done, John Montague's focus on "the struggle with casual / Graceless unheroic things," which entails "making poems out of the essentially unpoetic details of modern life" (Garratt 1986, 168) is to instance what divides Thomas Kinsella from poets like Montague and Heaney. In the poems considered in this chapter, Kinsella has come close to the operations of *Finnegans Wake,* where self both dissolves in and is constituted by language and scene: for many Kinsellan poems to come, language is the mode of existence of self. And in tracing/asserting the conception that the way language works can parallel the way the mind works, and that both parallel the way the world *is,* Kinsella's later work asserts the continuity of the "literary" and the ontological and addresses more and more vigorously the possibility of poetry as a way of knowing.

6. Quoted from *Kavanaugh's Weekly,* 24 May, 1952, p. 2, in Garratt 1986, 147.

7. The various versions of "The Irish Writer" are consistent in retaining Kinsella's conviction that while Yeats, by rising above the "filthy modern tide," stands for "the Irish tradition as broken, Joyce stands for it as continuous, or healed—or healing—from its mutilation" (Kinsella 1970, 65), and this just by virtue of Joyce's "relationship with the modern world," which is "direct and intimate." Despite those last phrases, Kinsella's remarks do not sound like an admiration of Joyce based on any putative preoccupation with the little things of life for their own sake pure and simple.

What we are beginning to see at this point in Kinsella's career—and we shall see more of it in the next chapter—is the productive convergence of certain influences. Some, like the influence of Joyce, come in part from outside (though that is a clumsy term), but there is one major impulse to development that cannot be so described. If my invoking the concept of a middle term is really applicable in attempting to account for these changes, it may be that the best candidate for the term is not "Phoenix Park" after all, but Kinsella's labors at translation that bore major fruit in his great rendition of the *Táin Bo Cuailnghe,* which was published by Dolmen in 1969, the year during which Kinsella says most of the poems in *Notes from the Land of the Dead* were composed.[8] His introduction to the *Táin* shows how much study went into the task of translating and makes it doubtful that the whole project was ever quite the marginal or casual thing he has claimed it was at first. Be that as it may, translation by its very nature presents the translator with an object that must be rendered in its own terms, whatever that might mean, but also in the terms of—*literally* in the terms of—the translator. The translation of a poetic text, possibly of any text, *requires* what I have described earlier as the opening to each other of scene—here the text—and self. Ezra Pound long ago asserted the essential similarity of translation and "original" composition (Pound 1970, 85): in both cases the mind comes upon something it wishes to render in its own terms, though to do so it must escape the rigidity of merely conventional (in every sense) expression. Bound by the "reality" of the text to be translated, the translator must nonetheless present his or her own rendition, which is for Pound the prototypical poetic situation: "Shall two know the same in their knowing?" he asks in the *Cantos.*

Confronting the Irish texts of the *Táin,* Kinsella was confronting the gap, the "broken tradition" of which he had written in "The Irish Writer" and "The Divided Mind"—confronting but also bridging it, and a necessary condition for that bridging was the deep rapprochement of self and scene. The early Kinsellan stance, "cold-blooded, simply the blank stare, the noting down of the event and allowing the poem and the reader to take their own conclusions" (Orr 1966, 106) is manifestly impossible for any serious attempt at translating.

Kinsella did speak of the *Táin* project as something fairly casual at first and said as late as his translator's note to the published work that it was "very much an aside to other things"; but he described the project

8. See the acknowledgment to the Guggenheim Foundation at the end of the Cuala Press edition of *NLD.*

ultimately as "an act of responsibility. . . . It's also the best way I know of appreciating the work itself. *The Táin* is part of our imaginative bedrock" (Haffenden 1981, 112). In other words, the *Táin* as scene opens itself to the committed translator, who in turn must open himself to the work, in "an act of loyalty to that part of one's own past." Nor is "scene" here only figurative. *Táin Bo Cuailnghe* comprises groups of tales from various ancient eras covering events of half a dozen centuries, and it comes down to us in various forms in manuscripts separated by centuries. To "objective" view it presents a heap of broken images; to translate it as Kinsella has done is an act of apprehension and recovery. The metaphor of bedrock is not the metaphor of a traditional lyric spectator but of a poet-participant in something like "Hand of Solo," where what is deeply seen is part of the speaker, who in turn is part of what is seen. A great poet is, among other things, a person on whom nothing is lost, and in Kinsella's transactions with his culture, with Joyce and Jung, and with Irish literature of the distant past (he went on, of course, to assemble *An Duanaire*, an anthology of Irish poetry accompanied by translations into English), he was consolidating an ever more profound ability to take things in.

But like the experiences that were to be the subject matter of poems in *A Technical Supplement* a few years later, this issue breaks up into others. The role of translation in the development of Kinsella's specifically literary abilities is only part of the story, for the fuller implications of which we must reach ahead, to his comments in the introduction of *The Oxford Book of Irish Verse*, where we find him writing that "For the modern Irish writer [the tradition of Irish poetry] now provides, after more than a century of retrieval and self-analysis, as living a link with the significant past as any stable, monolingual tradition could do, and the with the possibility of great richness and scope of reference" (Kinsella 1986, xxviii). The tradition suffered a devastating split between Irish and English, but "It should be clear," Kinsella says, "that the . . . tradition is a matter of two major bodies of poetry asking to be understood together as functions of a shared and painful history." He adds that to neglect either of those two components "is to miss a rare opportunity: that of responding to a notable and venerable literary tradition, the oldest vernacular literature in Western Europe, as it survives a change of vernacular."

This is a considerable change from the state of mind that lamented in 1970 that in the heritage of the Irish literary past "I recognize simultaneously a great inheritance and a great loss. The inheritance is mine, but only at two enormous removes—across a century's silence and through an exchange of worlds" (Kinsella 1970, 59). Translation is one way of alleviating that silence, though not perfectly: that can never be, at least not for the early Kinsella. The death of the Irish language—or, if one prefers, the suspension of its life for upwards of a century and a half—left a rift that no translation can ever bridge. The politics of conquest interrupted the natural growth of the language, and history necessarily left it behind. The English that breaks the silence is not the language that was silenced, and translation in such a context is simultaneously an attempt to recover and an acknowledgment that the loss is irretrievable.

And yet for the Kinsellan poet translation is an absolute necessity. Until speech is restored to his past, the poet is confined to the merest superficies of experience, rootless, almost totally without a history, and confined to whatever cultural purview the dominant culture in its magnanimous grandeur may see fit to grant him, or whatever of the domestic ambience can be made his own. Translation, then, is to be seen as a political—or, to use a term we shall see again, a *communitarian* act—and we confront here another aspect of Kinsella's dissolution of the conventional bonds of lyric, the linking of the literary act with history. The silence that translation attempts to break is not only literary: King John's castle, we might recall, "held speechless under its cold a whole province of Meath," and its ruined walls enclose "phases of void, Submarine silence."

What is locked in silence, moreover, is not only lost but *unexamined*, and that can mean *unconfronted*. Jung has pointed out that what we refuse to confront consciously we are usually forced to confront unconsciously. The immediate bearing of this on a more or less puritanical Catholic culture such as Ireland's is obvious enough. Some things are not done, and even more are not talked about. (Of her version of the *Táin* Lady Gregory wrote, "I left out a good deal I thought you would not care about for one reason or another."[9]

Moreover, the silence that envelopes the Irish tradition was itself created by violence, by extermination, by genocide; and later, when genocide was being aided by the natural calamity of the Famine, the living speech of Gaels was further silenced by the tally sticks hung around the necks of Irish schoolchildren, for each lapse into Irish a notch and a concomitant educative beating. Recuperation through translation is perhaps a way of healing, in part, the damage done by such violence to the Irish past and Irish spirit. The violence cannot be undone by any act of reclamation no matter how pious; but to regain in any measure that which violence ripped away may contribute to a partial healing of the victim and may stand as at least a limited restitution.

In a positive light, to be able to reach into the *Lebor Gabála Erenn*,

9. Quoted in Kinsella 1969, xiv.

the Book of the Takings of Ireland, and adapt a chant of Amargin sancti-
fying the Milesian arrival in Ireland, to appropriate in English another
text, about the four rivers of Paradise, as in "Nuchal" from *Notes from the
Land of the Dead*—to do these things is to declare the viable oneness in
time of the Irish experience. In a useful negative light, if that is what it
should be called, it is as if the treacheries and bloodiness of tales like the
Exile of the Sons of Usnech and the *Táin* were a kind of archetype against
which to assess the paltry shenanigans of more modern Irish public figures
—as in the tawdry history of political intrigue Kinsella sets forth in the
satiric tale of Fox and Groom in "Nightwalker." Myths or legends brought
over into English through translation function for Kinsella, that is, as
for Joyce and Pound: they furnish eternal patterns or categories whose
deployment renders coherent the vagaries of history ancient and modern,
and they place the poet, by the act of translation, and the reader, by the
act of reception, in a finally, at long last continuous stream of historical
experience. All of these considerations have an obvious bearing on
Kinsella's move away from the limitations of the conventional lyric. Seeking to empower a self other than the pragmatist's, and to shore up the
status of poetry in a philistine and rationalist age, W. B. Yeats had fanta-
sized that an emotional impulse in a Greek shepherd lad might eventuate
centuries later in a battlefield cataclysm. Such fancies would perhaps seem
blasphemous to a poet who had come to maturity during the Second
World War. But must the facts of history arrogate all value and discount
all other ways of knowing? What if world and self, like Einstein's matter
and energy, stand in a coordinate relation rather than a relation of prior-
ity? And what might come of a lyric poetry grounded in the notion that
fact might be an aspect of mind, to some practical intents and purposes
the external replication (though not necessarily the *result*) of psychic patterns? For such questions to be realistic, the concept of an extension of
the poetic self has to be more than notional. How well grounded that idea
was in Kinsella's poetics, both conceptually and in terms of creditable
realization in the flesh and blood of verse, will be the next focus of inquiry.

4   (Re)Forming the Self

What I'm trying to do in *Notes from the Land of the Dead*," Kinsella has said, is "to start almost before consciousness and let the dawning of individuation control what will happen. . . . I will get those stories [from Irish myth] actually into the poetry in a dramatic way, almost certainly by having the undefined consciousness, which is at the root of the poems in *Notes*, becoming more defined . . . so that the thing will have a dramatic effect and gather up the mythical Irish contents of the subconscious" (O'Hara 1981, 7–8).

His further remark that "A poet produces his poems almost as by-products of his attempts to come to terms with his own significance" and that the poem itself is "evidence that a further stage in the continuous act of understanding has been reached" (O'Hara 1981, 12) implies that the poems are to be read primarily with reference to the mind of the poet, and this might not at first glance suggest much of an opening out of the poet's scope. But in these remarks he collocates, with the implicit aid of Jacobi and Jung, the three importantly related entities: self, myth, and unconscious.

The Jungian concept of *individuation,* so casually passed along, as it seems, in the remarks to O'Hara, was a powerful component in the new developments of Kinsella's aesthetic. In Jung, individuation is the process of coming into genuine selfhood, "the better and more complete fulfillment of the collective qualities of the human being." Its negative aim is "to divest the self of the false wrappings of the persona on the one hand, and of the suggestive power of the primordial images on the other" (Jung

87

1966, 184.)[1] The desideratum is the capacity to draw on the nutritive and energizing impulses of the unconscious without being overwhelmed by them and at the same time not to fall into a neurotic defense against them by deploying a narrow and fanatic ego. The goal is an expansion of the self in at least two senses: by its rapprochement with unconscious impulses the self is effectively enlarged beyond the narrowly restrictive bounds dictated by its conscious aspects—the *persona* in one terminology, the skills of getting and spending in another. But because the unconscious is ultimately communal and both sub- and transhistorical, the self that can assimilate it becomes something more than the fortuitous and powerless entity it is in the early Kinsella. The process leads not to the "individualism" of a pointless rebellion or self-assertion, but the attainment by the individual of his or her "unique combination, or gradual differentiation, of functions and faculties which in themselves are universal."[2] In distinguishing individuation from mere egocentricity, Jung proposes that connectedness, not boundedness, characterizes the fully realized self; to explore an authentic self is therefore to explore more than "personality" or a bounded "individualism," since to be bounded precludes being a real individual. Technically described, individuation according to Jacobi (again, the principal source in Kinsella's initial introduction to Jungian theories) involves three processes: the experiencing of the *shadow,* that repository of aspects of the ego unwelcome for whatever reason to consciousness; confrontation with the *anima/animus,* the contrasexual opposite beneath every consciousness; and finally a confrontation with a central archetypal figure, the "old wise man" in men, and the Magna Mater in women. Passage through these three stages will under the best conditions culminate in self-realization through the union of the various pairs of potentialities, masculine and feminine, conscious and unconscious—and most important at this point in discussion, individual and communal.

1. Compare, from Jung's "Psychological Approach to the Dogma of the Trinity":

Self-reflection or—what amounts to the same thing—the urge towards individuation gathers together what is scattered and multifarious and exalts it to the original form of the One, the Primordial Man. In this way our existence as separate beings, our former ego nature, is abolished, the circle of consciousness is widened, and because the paradoxes have been made conscious the sources of conflict are dried up (Jung 1969, 265).

2. Individuation is thus partly a moral and social process by means of which one is "truly able to form a community, i.e., to be an integral part of a group of human beings, and not merely a cipher in the mass" (Jacobi 1951, 140) and partly something metaphysical: to awaken the energy in the unconscious "to new life and to integrate it with consciousness means . . . nothing less than to take the individual out of his isolation and to incorporate him in the eternal cosmic process" (Jacobi 1951, 64).

Kinsella by no means writes allegories on Jungian themes, but all of these stages figure in his later work. The strategies in "Phoenix Park" that extend the transcendent powers of both the self and the lyric already draw on Jung's operations and theories. Jung's conception that psychic life is a vital interplay of opposites ("Energy presupposes . . . pre-existent antithesis, without which there can be no energy at all" [Jung 1966, 75])[3] is practically an incitement to propose a counteractive force to a perceived principle of entropy, and Kinsella was already making such proposals on his own, as we have seen. In "Phoenix Park" and its contemporaries, especially "Nightwalker," he was developing just such a sense of the self as a meaningful counterweight to the aimless, entropic welter of history. To establish such a sense on grounds of "value" or desire or wish would have been easy but ineffectual: the valued can perish as easily as the hated. The Yeats-like enterprise in "Phoenix Park" and now in *Notes from the Land of the Dead* is to redefine the self in such a way as to ensure not just its private security but its substantial value. To this end, the confluence of Jung with a number of other significant forces in Kinsella's developing poetics was a powerful aid. Conceptually speaking, one important confluence was the inevitable pairing of Jung and Irish myth.

In "The High Road" the suggestive assimilation of the young boy at the "Robbers' Den" to the legendary figure of Tuan/Fintan, for example, has the same implication in Kinsella as the assimilation of any self to any myth does in Jung. As a rudimentary manifestation of a Jungian feminine principle (more specifically, an aspect of *anima*) and given the poet's reference to her as "the all-swallowing hag" (O'Hara 1981, 16), the grandmother in "Tear" and "A Hand of Solo" echoes a whole gallery of Celtic myth figures—Morrighan, the goddess of slaughter; the earth-goddess Mebh; the Minerva-like Brigid; and Sheela-na-gig, the terrible-mother manifestation of Gaea Mater, among others.[4] To what one might term the horizontal continuities Kinsella was asserting for the self and its experiences, his use of Jung and the related rapprochement with myth adds a vertical resonance, underscoring the historicality or historicity of individualist experiences through their replications of the past. Jung's conceptions

3. Cf. "The Problem of the Attitude-Type": "there is no energy unless there is a tension of opposites; hence it is necessary to discover the opposite to the attitude of the conscious mind." (Jung 1966, 53).

4. See Sharkey 1975, 8, and MacCana 1970, 85–90. The Sheela-na-Gig is a grotesque effigy depicting a disproportionately large head surmounting a small torso, parted legs, and a capacious vulva held open by the figure's hands. Carvings of this figure ornament churches and castles alike in Ireland and England. (Sharkey's example is on the corbel of the Church of St. Mary and St. David in Kilpeck, Herefordshire, and there is one on the parish church at Ballyvourney, where Kinsella's friend Seán O'Riada is buried.)

of the vital historicity of the psyche are well known: "Inner peace and contentment depend in large measure upon whether or not the historical family which is inherent in the individual can be harmonized with the ephemeral conditions of the present" (Jung 1961, 237). The self's very participation in history is a major component of its reality and certainly of its welfare: "The less we understand of what our fathers and fore-fathers sought the less we understand ourselves, and thus we help with all our might to rob the individual of his roots and his guiding instincts, so that he becomes a particle in the mass, ruled only by what Nietzsche called the spirit of gravity" (Jung 1961, 236). The reasoning behind these assertions leads to the concept of the collective unconscious: "Our souls as well as our bodies are composed of individual elements which were already present in the ranks of our ancestors. . . . Body and soul have an intensely historical character and find no proper place in what is new, in things that have just come into being" (Jung 1961, 235).

One need not accept that nebulous concept on its own terms; to the extent that Jung's line of thought points to a substantial continuity between self and historical community—and contributes further grounding to the mutual opening of self and scene—it need not matter how the idea is founded. Admittedly, to historicize the self is not to empower it. But support for that aspect of Kinsella's developing concept of the capabilities of the self could also be found in Jungian thought—specifically, for example, in Jacobi's quotation of Jung's friend and collaborator, Toni Wolff:

> The irreversibility characteristic of dynamic processes in lifeless nature [Jacobi writes] can be canceled only by . . . interfering with the natural order and compelling it to a reversal. . . . "It pertains to the creativeness of the psyche that interference in the mere natural order constitutes its very being. The creation of consciousness and the possibility of differentiating and broadening consciousness are its principal act of interference," the source of its power to control and compel nature. (Jacobi 1951, 73)

Remarks like these constitute a clear invitation to conceive of mind or the self as interactive, and Kinsella was ready to follow.

Still, to know about Jung and about myth is not the same as being able to write about, or even after the style of, either one. For a poet, in fact, "not to be able to write about" may be tantamount to not really knowing. The enabling experience for this aspect of Kinsella's work was his move to America in 1963 and his assimilation of the examples of Pound and William Carlos Williams. Like many non-American writers of

English, Kinsella missed the merits of Williams—until he confronted his work on Williams's home ground. "For a non-American," he has said,

> it used to be easy to accept and enjoy Wallace Stevens while dismissing Williams as mere prose. But, hearing the American voice in Williams, listening to him in the American accent, let me take the poetry straight and understand it. That, once I got it, was the single most helpful thing. . . . It's been a sort of leverage out of a rather clamped tradition—with very few exits for poetry—into a state of thinking, an attitude where anything is possible. (O'Hara 1981, 6)

Whereas the influence of Auden and Yeats in Kinsella's early work was almost exclusively stylistic ("all those superficial things" was Kinsella's characterization to John Haffenden of what had appealed to him in Auden), the effect of his study of Pound and Williams, like the effect of Joyce and Jung, was structural, attitudinal, and conceptual. Instead of verbal echoes of Auden or Yeats—or any other echoes—we find a version of Pound's and Joyce's juxtapository method and a stance within poems that reflects the complex observational pose of Williams. "I'm . . . grateful to the work of Ezra Pound and William Carlos Williams," he said,

> for having opened up particular lines of style—not by any means for imitation, but revelations of scope and attitude—and (particularly in Williams's case) of a kind of creative relaxation in the face of complex reality; to remain open, "prehensile," not rigidly committed. . . . The response becomes one's life-work, rather than a sequence of individual poems. (Haffenden 1981, 106)

"Particular lines of style" seems at first a rather anomalous companion to "revelations of scope and attitude," but what Kinsella is pointing to here is the fact that those two poets contributed to his ability to use—to *write*—what he gained from Jung, and from them. *Scope* and *attitude* are shorthand for the capabilities of a poetic self akin to what I have so far attributed to Kinsella's reading in Jung. The remarks to Haffenden are so perfectly in keeping with the vigorously acceptive and interactive stance toward experience promulgated by Jung that the two sets of influences have to be seen as going together in Kinsella's development. If Jung suggested or revealed to the poet the hitherto unsuspected extent of the resonance of personal and public experiences, Jung's, Pound's, and Williams's attitudes toward experience must together have been part of what encouraged him to the "kind of creative relaxation in the face of complex reality" that distinguishes *Notes from the Land of the Dead* from *Night-walker*. Experiences cease to be regarded as a series of end-stopped events such as "Phoenix Park" is a move away from, events whose significance is either momentaneously dramatic or perhaps personally striking. Williams had moved beyond the events he could constate in the conventional lyric well before he undertook the deeper and more inclusive scope of *Paterson*. Already, in the early poem "Spring Strains," Williams vigorously redefines the nature of the observed scene, opening *fact* to the revelations of the poetic self: as the sun is reformed into a string of concepts, the entire scene is redefined as a seemingly Cubist painting:

> But—
> (Hold hard, rigid jointed trees)
> the blinding and red-edged sun-blur—
> creeping energy, concentrated
> counterforce—welds sky, buds, trees,
> rivets them in one puckering hold!
> Sticks through! Pulls the whole
> counter-pulling mass upward, to the right
> locks even the opaque, not yet defined
> ground in a terrific drag that is
> loosening the very tap roots!
>   (Williams 1988, 97)

No poetic operation could be more unlike the work of the early Kinsella —unless it is the Irish poet's own late work. Pound, too, had to move beyond lyric, with all that the phrase implies, to reach the comprehensiveness of the *Cantos*. Implicit in Kinsella's remark that "the response becomes one's life-work, rather than a sequence of individual poems" is something akin to the revision in Pound's conception of the poetic act in his evolution from Imagism to the theories of Vorticism—the move, that is, from the concept of the poet as perceptive to the idea of the poetic mind as *con*ceptive, not passively "perceiving forms," as he put it, but actively conceiving, shaping reality according to the actually *cognitive* powers of the creative imagination.[5] The change is reflected in the interview-language references to the poetic process Kinsella made in the interview with Haffenden, where he sees himself as directed by "the impulse merely to understand, not to impose order," and in his remark that the changed tone of his poems may reflect that "nicer things are happening to me—or

5. See Jackson 1968, 100–110.

maybe the act of understanding gives one a larger attitude" (Haffenden 1981, 109). He is speaking reticently of developments utterly central to his work: a point where experiences and things of personal significance radiate outward and where external things—Jung, for example, and the poetry of Pound and Williams—converge. The mutual opening, as I have termed it, of self and scene takes on, then, a complex and comprehensive significance.

If he was ever in any sense a localist poet, Kinsella here definitively ceases to be one, turning to kinds and treatments of experience unlike anything his Irish contemporaries were dealing with. For one thing, the idea that the loss and violence in human history must be accepted simply as what happens becomes plainly intolerable—as the related view that persons simply do what they do is rejected as vacuous. Given loss and violence, Kinsella comes to ask, is there no coherent genesis, no sense to be made, nothing to do but lament? Like Wordsworth in *The Prelude*, he comes to see the problems of poetry as in part the problems of life (the problems of the "Ireland" of writers he perhaps had seen from the start as problems of humanity). Tentatively in *Nightwalker* and irretrievably in *Notes from the Land of the Dead* he performs a move unparalleled, so far as I know, in twentieth-century poetry, entering a decade-long process of exploration, the exploration and the writing of a self so radically abstract from one point of view and so utterly basic from another that the twin dangers of a doctrinaire Jungianism and a sometimes alienating obscurity could and did threaten his immediate public standing as reviewer after reviewer threw up his hands at the work after *Nightwalker*.[6] He put at risk his popularity, the audience it had taken years to win—all for the sake of the integrity of his art.

Yet those often strange poems in *Notes from the Land of the Dead*, shuttling back and forth as they do between the seemingly everyday and the seemingly fantastic, pursue their own kind of realism. They are embarked on a decidedly non-Wordsworthian mode of self-exploration. For, though I have characterized the poems as forming an integrated book, the book

---

6. Calvin Bedient, for one (*New York Times Book Review*, 16 June 1974), 4, saw *Notes from the Land of the Dead* as mainly fragments whose various ellipses had no discernible point. "The dream poems," he felt, "are conceptually tired" and "his new poems merely *bear*." David Bromwich was even more helplessly dismissive in his review in *Poetry* for January 1975. Vernon Young in *Parnassus* (Spring/Summer 1975) and Alisdan Madian in *The Listener* (1973) were almost alone in their intelligent grasp of what Kinsella might be up to.

is very much part of a continuing process—it proclaims its link with *Nightwalker* in the epigraph quoted from the last four lines of "Phoenix Park,"

> A snake out of the void moves in my mouth, sucks
> a triple darkness. A few ancient faces
> detach and begin to circle. Deeper still,
> delicate distinct tissue begins to form,
>
> (*N*, 84)

and asserts its link with work to come by the inclusion of two poems that would reappear five years later as integral components of *Peppercanister Poems*, "Butcher's Dozen" and "A Selected Life."

Reviewers might have taken comfort in the unexceptionable clarity of the last of the "Other Poems" in the American edition, "Wyncote, Pennsylvania: A Gloss":

> A mocking-bird on a branch
> outside the window, where I write,
> gulps down a wet crimson berry,
> shakes off a few bright drops
> from his wing, and is gone
> into a thundery sky.
>
> Another storm coming.
> Under that copper light
> my papers seem luminous.
> And over them I will take
> ever more painstaking care.
>
> (*NLD*, 71)

The speaker is obviously in full possession of his daylight world, proposing, like the characteristic Kinsella speaker, earnest work and going about his proper poet's business of taking his cue from a bird: like Keats and Shelley, like Yeats and Williams.

But the poem of course gathers up the sequence of experiences that make up the rest of the book. The writing self of this poem has canvassed, and must be seen as colored by, a variety of other selves, some plainly fictive ("Worker in Mirror, At His Bench," "Death Bed," "Sacrifice") some less so (the Darwinian voice of "St. Paul's Rocks: 16 February 1832"), and some relatively autobiographical ("The Route of the Táin," "The High Road," and others), the whole constitutive of a confident but not mindlessly comfortable pursuit of individuation in its fullest, Jungian, sense. The daylight-world images of bird, berry, drop, and ingestion are heavy with the resonance of their counterparts in earlier contexts less brightly lit. Why? What has been gained? And in what sense is the poem "A Gloss"?

It is a gloss on the rest of the book,[7] in that the term is an invitation to weigh the other poems in the light of this, and this in the light of the others. In a way, this is the lee shore gained, gained not without cost. The bird is a domestication of the murderous owl in "At the Crossroads," and upon the vow that over his luminous-seeming papers "I will take ever more painstaking care," the horrors passed through in earlier poems confer a highly moving intensity.

The process glossed is grounded in the interrelations between the prologue-like "hesitate, cease to exist, glitter again" and "Hen Woman." It is initiated by the irony-laden Faustian descent that opens the current version of the collection.[8] Twentieth-century Fausts must do without Mephistophelian mentors, and Faustian laboratory gadgets turn out to be the paraphernalia of mundane breakfasts:

> Many a time
> I have risen from my gnawed books
> and prowled about, wrapped in a long grey robe,
> and rubbed my forehead; reached for my instruments
> —canister and kettle, the long-handled spoon,
> metal vessels and delph; settled the flame,
> blue and yellow and, in abstracted hunger,
> my book propped before me, eaten forkfuls
> of scrambled egg and buttered fresh bread
> and taken hot tea until the sweat stood out
> at the roots of my hair!
>
> (*NLD*, 3)

The magical key that was Faust's *entrée* into the underworld of the Mothers here to be more like the male member standing ready for masturbation (unless the image is not penis, but pen):

7. But note as well: "The main reference of "Gloss" [in "Wyncote, Pennsylvania: A Gloss"] is those old monastic glosses in Irish, near the beginning of the *New Oxford Book [of Irish Verse]* (p. 30)" (TK, letter of 21 Jan. 1994.)

8. The Cuala Press edition of *Notes from the Land of the Dead* opened with a fairly programmatically Jungian "Prologue" that did seem to recount the poet's confrontation with the *anima*. It seems overtly Jungian indeed—which is perhaps why Kinsella excised it for the New York edition of these poems.

> I have lain down on the soiled divan
> alert as though for a journey
> and turned to things not right nor reasonable
> . . . .
> The key, though I hardly knew it,
>   already in my fist.
> Falling. Mind darkening.
>   Toward a ring of mouths.
>
> (*NLD*, 4)

Irony-laden or not, this initiates a series of recurrent descents into a subra-tional darkness on which the organization of the book turns—a handful of poems that expose the primitive issues on which the more conscious-world poems in this volume are founded, and at the same time loosely recapitulate stages in the speaker's development toward personhood. The dream vision of this prologue recounts an experience the exact nature of which it skills not to ask. The poet's humdrum teakettle is transmogrified into the Celto-Faustian cauldron from which "a vapour of forms curdled, glittered and vanished," and surrounding which he sees "a ring . . . of naked ancient women." The cauldron, a ubiquitous item in Irish myth and history, is resonant testimony to the extended significance of the self and its experiences.[9] Other categories likewise dissolve, extend into the primordial past, reform, and in general resist the assumption of stability. What the poet is envisioning could be an experience of the grave, or a fantasy of consciousness in the womb, as in

> . . . countless forms drifting as I did,
> Wavery albumen bodies
> each burdened with an eye.

A half-dozen or so lines are reminiscent of the first scene of *Paradise Lost:*

> Poor spirits!
> How tentative and slack our search

    9. The most famous mythic cauldron was that of the Celtic god Dagda, "from which no company ever went away unsatisfied" (MacCana 1970, 66), but another remarkable one was the cauldron the monstrous Formorians used to feed the Dagda himself; they filled it with eighty gallons of milk and "the like quantity of meal and fat." He was forced to eat it all up on pain of death; such are the Dagda's appetites that he was fully content to do so. See, among other tellings, Cross 1936, 39, "The Second Battle of Mag Tured." Not unnatu-rally, the cauldron was an item of importance in the household furnishings of *boaires* or freemen. See also Byrne 1967.

> along the dun shore whose perpetual hiss
> breaks softly, and breaks again,
> on endless broken shells!
>
> (*NLD*, 5)

Earlier passages suggest Dante in the underworld. In the end the poem gathers up all these implicated, concentric energies and announces its dramatic and thematic function as the psychic preparation for the poems to follow:

> How it was done—that that pot should now
> be boiling before you . . .
> . . . .
>   . . . you shall have . . .
>
> —what shall we not begin
> to have, on the
>   count of
>   0
>
>   (*NLD*,5)

The first poem of the section "an egg of being," "Hen Woman," purports to have happened in the factual world, and it handles the same leading images—the content of the ironically shaded psychomachia of the prologue is projected into the world of public physical event. The speaker watches the laying of an egg which, falling from the hen, eludes the grasp of its owner and "smashed against the grating. . . . The soft mucous shell clung a little longer, then drained down," even as the dreamer of the prologue fell "in my shell of solitude" through "certain bars of iron laid down side by side" until he "scattered in a million droplets." The laying of the egg

> The black zero of the orifice
> closed to a point
> and the white zero of the egg hung free
>   (*NLD*, 10)

is a transform of the woman emerging from her house:

> The cottage door opened,
> a black hole

> in a whitewashed wall so bright
> the eyes narrowed
>
> (*NLD*, 9)

as the whole event is a transform of the obscure vision of the prologue. We seem to have parentheses within parentheses: the woman emerging from the doorway is the egg emerging from the sphincter, which is the poet falling into vision, and the whole is the imaginative experience emerging from the poet as the poem, as the whole book "emerges" from this poem:

> I feed upon it still, as you see;
> there is no end to that which,
> not understood, may yet be noted
> and hoarded in the imagination,
> in the yolk of one's being, so to speak,
> there to undergo its (quite animal) growth,
> . . . .
> Something that had—clenched
> in its cave—not been
> now was: an egg of being[10]
>
> (*NLD*, 11)

The speaker's translation of the old woman's dismissive "It's all the one" into the Gnostic slogan, *"Hen to pan,"*[11] is Kinsella's now characteristic

----

10. Cf. "Thus the non-existent God made a non-existent universe out of the non-existent, establishing and giving substance to one certain seed which had within it the whole semination of the universe. It is like the egg of some variegated . . . bird . . . an egg which though one has within it many forms of multiform, many-colored, many-consituted substances" (Grant 1961, 126, paraphrasing the Gnostic writer Basilides).

11. Rosenberg 1980, 270; she identifies the phrase as a Gnostic inscription beneath depictions of the ouroboros. An example from a fourteenth-century alchemical text can be seen in Rudolph 1983, 70. Gnosticism seems also to be the source of the term *Urmensch* in the early poem "Downstream" (above, p. 26). According to Rudolph (1983, 71–72), this figure in Gnostic cosmological theory "meets the attack of darkness at the behest of the king of light and introduces the cosmological development"—that is, the creation of the (by definition evil) world. Gnostic conceptions of the feminine also parallel, along with the concepts of Jung, the ambiguity of the feminine in Kinsella's work. One Gnostic school ascribed the creation of the physical world to the feminine presence Pistis (faith); elsewhere the feminine is seen as a redemptive figure. The snake that sucks a triple darkness at the outset of *Notes from the Land of the Dead* is another Gnostic concept rhyme, complete with ambiguity, since in Gnostic thought the serpent was both evil and, in the form of the ouroboros, the mystic snake, protective and ultimately an embodiment of the redemptive. See Walker 1983, 905–909, for a discussion of the serpent that is highly suggestive in relation to Kinsella's work.

rejection of the boundary between the psychic or imaginative and the physical. The facts of "Hen Woman" were given in a remembered childhood event; their congruence with the psychic events of the "Hesitate, cease to exist" lines is structured, written, by the poetic imagination of the author, and this is a new thing for Kinsella's poetry. As the lyric materials of "Phoenix Park" open out into issues beyond the lyrical, so here the inner adventures of a self open into parallels with the outer. Obviously the vision postdates the experience of "Hen Woman"; it comes, we might say with Jung, to remind the poet of his unfinished business with whatever it was in the "Hen Woman" episode he unwittingly registered as pregnant with significance.

The reminder speaks true, for the sometimes hidden but always central focus of this whole volume is the poet's confrontation, in a gripping adaptation of the technicalities of the Jungian concept of individuation, with the nurturing and threatening mystery of the Feminine. The concept is Jungian, but whether we call it the poet's Shadow or his Anima—or his Typewriter—matters little; as Kinsella conceives of the creative process, what is at issue is in any case a powerful though unexplored aspect of himself and his history, a side of his psyche which, like everyone, he must eventually open to consciousness. On the level of consciousness itself, the process is one in which as he developed toward a creative selfhood the poet has had to assimilate the significance of various women, loving and yet often disquieting or downright frightening, who have played some part or other in his life. What is gradually discovered to him, one might say, is the way these humdrum human figures open out emotionally into deep resonances in the psyche: again, we are pursuing the process by which experiences take on meaning—and what meanings they take on.

The principal realistic agent of the mystery is, as we have seen, the poet's grandmother as seen with the eyes of his childhood. The bevy of powerful and ambiguous divinities with which the poems associate her helps explain the boy's fear of her and partly explains such gruesome outbursts of fantasy violence as the murderous vision of "Ely Place." Behind the speaker of "Survivor," Tuan or Fintan, is the legendary Cessair and the fifty women Fintan was assigned to service—or are those fifty women actually a bizarre one magnified into an anagram for frightening sexual voraciousness (what or whose psyche is revealed by the threatening indecency of Sheela-na-gig)? In any event there is in the Survivor's consciousness the figure of the Hag as well (*NLD*, 32), "squatting on the water, / her muzzle staring up at nothing." The grandmother, in her shop, is seated "on her high stool, chewing nothing." "You'd think I had three heads!" (*NLD*, 15) she jokes, unknowingly associating herself with a pan-

theon of triple goddesses of often fearsome aspect—Kali and the Morrighan, to name but two—[12] or Hecate, whose presence is implied by the
imagery of crossroads, dog's body, and owl in "At the Crossroads." The
grandmother, too, has a key, here and in "Ancestor," where "Her profile
against the curtains / was old, and dark like a hunting bird's," resembling
in this "Mrs. Fullerton . . . sitting on a stool in her doorway, / beak-nosed,
one eye dead" in "The High Road" (*NLD*, 16).

A similar resonance energizes "Tear," a poem in which the feminine
figures in more than one way. Sent in to see his dying ancestress, the boy
cannot bring himself either to weep or to kiss her. On the contrary, the
"stale abyss" that pressed its weird erotic aura upon his inarticulate sensibility reaches out for him even more threateningly here as he is "swallowed
in chambery dusk," and the odors of "snuff and musk" carry him off into
the myth-founded anxiety remarked upon earlier (p. 81), into "a derelict
place / smelling of ash: unseen walls and roofs / rustled like breathing;" as
the boy fuses with Fintan, the grandmother flows into an identity with
the Hag of "Survivor." But the grandmother also becomes the vehicle of
wisdom when she speaks of the weeping of the boy's father over the death
of their infant girl—another instance of a perishing feminine, this one
having called out the more fully manly (because more "feminine"?) response of expressed grief.

That Jung's attraction for Kinsella lay primarily along the lines of
method and not mere literalized doctrine is clear from the relationship of
these poems to what a more thoroughgoing Jungianism might call their
implicit psychic content. Jung was interested in the upwelling of psychic
forces manifested in *projection,* in which the lines of force generally run
from the inner repressed to the outer behavioral. Because Kinsella is interested not in expatiating on the unconscious invisible but, like Pound and
Williams, in understanding the visible, his lines of force generally run in
the direction opposite to Jung's. There are cases, however, where something akin to projection does seem to be on the poet's mind—"Ely Place,"
for example, and the curious manipulating of Irish myth in "Nuchal."

"Nuchal" draws on the description of the rivers of Paradise in the
Lebor Gabála Erenn's Irish translation of *Genesis* (Macalister 1938, 197).
The sleeping woman whose fingers dangling into the rivulet divide the
water into the Biblical Phison, Tigris, Euphrates, and Geon is not in
Genesis or the Irish translation, where "Nuchal" is the name of the original

12. See MacCana 1970, 85–87. For a brief but helpful comment on these figures, see
also Sharkey 1975, 7–9.

river, not of the sleeping woman. Kinsella's beautiful meditation on the original,

> Eastward, a quiet river feeds the soil
> till the soft banks crumble, caked with oil.
> A sudden shine, out of eternal spring:
> a crop of gold, with many a precious thing
> —bdellium, seeking the pearl in its own breast,
> the flower-figured onyx, the amethyst . . .
> (*NLD*, 28)

grew out of this workaday soil:

> As for Phison, [which is called the river
> of Ganges, eastward straight it goeth].
> It is that stream which surroundeth all
> the land of Euilath, that place where gold
> is generated, precious and most beautiful:
> and there is found bdellium, and the other
> precious stone which is called onyx.
> . . . .
> Phison a river of oil, gently eastward. . . .
> (Macalister 1938, 57, 197)

Yet the apparently serene beauty of his version is undercut by considerable irony: the sleeping woman's fingers trail "ladylike" in the water, and the southerly branch of the now-divided stream rolls to sweeten the salt marsh "to some degree"—such banalities are always a danger sign in Kinsella's discourse, as are the slips into poetic archaism toward the close: "Many a precious thing" and "Four rivers reaching toward th'encircling sea." The quotation marks that bracket the entire poem ascribe it to a non-Kinsellan poet less than fully conscious of his implicit ascription of the cause of danger and the loss of paradisal unity to the feminine. It as though Kinsella were satirizing his own conventional imagizing of the feminine: rapt in his vision of beauty, this speaker certainly projects onto the feminine a responsibility for such things as the implications of his own transformation of Macalister's *"Tigris wine"* into *"tigrish, through narrow gorges, winy red."*

This whole section of the book, *"a single drop,"* is largely a juxtapository construct of angles of vision on the feminine (and, as the adjective *juxtapository* implies, owes its method in some part to Kinsella's interest in Pound).[13] "Endymion" is a fragment narrated from the point of view of Luna (a manifestation of Hecate, and consequently related to the Irish Morrighan). "At the Crossroads," with its vision of the innocently murderous owl, Hecate's bird, is an implicit meditation on the feminine Shadow itself, and "Sacrifice" is a gruesome and self-deceptive satire on the Shadow or the Anima or a feminine principle—actually on a mode of discourse. The poet's claim (Haffenden 1981, 108) that "the distance between the narrator and protagonist has become enormous" is important and relates the poem to what I suggested about "Nuchal." Its cliché-ridden language is horribly out of keeping with its grisly imaginings:

> Never mind the hurt. I've never felt
> so terribly alive, so ready, so gripped
> by love—gloved fingers slippery
> next the heart!
>   Is it very difficult?
> . . . .
>   Are you stuck?
> Let me arch back.
> . . . .
> I love your tender triumph, straightening up
> lifting your reddened sleeves. The stain
>   spreads   downward
> through your great flushed pinions.
> You are a real angel.
> My heart is in your hands: mind it well.
>   (*NLD*, 36–37)

The grotesque inadequacy of language to event here is obviously the inadequacy of *response* to event, the point of the poem. In the work of a

---

13. It is not unfair to point out, I think, that a major vitalization of Kinsella's work correlates with this turn to specifically American models. The centrifugal development of literature in English has become increasingly striking as this century has progressed. With the one exception of Lawrence, the energy in prose fiction in this century has been located in non-British centers—Ireland, Africa, the United States. The major migration of poetry got under way at about the same time. That there is no British counterpart to Pound, Eliot, Stevens, or Williams has been obvious for some time. What is striking is that there has been no British equivalent even of talents like Ammons, Duncan, Ginsberg, or Ashbery. Kenner (1988) builds a gloomy *capriccio* around this very subject. Certainly a poet of Kinsella's abilities could not respond for long to a siren song so limited as Auden's.

poet who has been preoccupied with violence to the extent Kinsella has, such goings-on must be a danger to be distanced with all possible vigor, which in a way is what is going on here. The survivor's inability to articulate disasters and loss we have already seen, and the unutterable fears of the poet as a boy have been put forth in "A Hand of Solo" and "Ancestor." In a weird enough way, "Sacrifice" thrusts such linguistic inadequacies as far away and as violently as possible, projecting them onto a transsexual counterpart of the poet whose fears they really are.

"An egg of being," then, is a Poundian disposition of ultimately inadequate projections (projections are always inadequate, according to Jung, for they illegitimately confuse the outer with the inner), and if one credits the poet's move among a series of *personae* as dramatic exploration, the poems can be seen as an externalized pursuit of a stance—a stance toward some vague threat that he has not yet recognized as coming from himself. The low point of this drama of self-deception, if that is what it is, is the astonishing savagery in "Ely Place." But that poem is preceded by the low point of coherent consciousness in *Notes from the Land of the Dead*, the eerie dream of "All Is Emptiness and I Must Spin," which opens the section *"nightnothing."* Its content if not its tone makes the experience of "hesitate, cease to exist, glitter again" seem child's play by comparison, and its language is a strange blending of private and public terrors. What the poem most seems to designate is a dream:

> A vacancy in which apparently
> I hang
>   with severed senses
>
>   .
>
> I have been in places . . .
>   (*NLD*, 41)

But not all the speaker's observations seem to fit such a reading: "How bring oneself to judge, or think," he asks, "so hurled onward! / Inward!" And the shifting tenses seem to shuttle us between an account of a dream and the musings of a dazed latter-day Faust awakening from his journey to the Mothers:

> After a while, in the utter darkness,
> there was a slight but perceptible
> movement of the air.
> It was not Death, but Night. . .
> . . . .

> A distant door
> clangs. Echo of voices.
>
>   .
>
> The sterile: it is a whole matter in itself.
> Fantastic millions of
> fragile
>
> in every single
>
> (*NLD*, 42)

Or are some of the events in the dream—the clang of the door, for example—a reminiscence of German death camps?

> We were made to separate
> and strip. My urine flowed
> with mild excitement.
> Our hands touched lightly
> in farewell.
>
> (*NLD*, 41)

At the very least, or the very most, the poem can be taken as a revision of "hesitate, cease to exist, glitter again": an ideogram-like inscription of the altered sensibility of the compiler of these juxtaposed experiences. And it may not be incidental that in place of the semijocular and initially person-alized appeals to Faust and myth in the earlier poem we have here a string of images that shimmer with horrendous political possibilities—as the "tears of self forming" may echo the state of unformed humanity evinced by the young boy of "Tear," who could not weep.

The poem does not "prepare for" "Ely Place" novelistically; the strat-egy continues to follow the methods of Pound and Williams in the *Cantos* and *Paterson*. The gruesome central scene

> A blood vision
> started out of the brick: the box
> of keys in my pocket—I am opening it,
> tongue-tied. I unpick the little
> pen-knife and dig it in her throat,
> her spirting gullet!
>
> (*NLD*, 44)

is related to the concerns of "Sacrifice" the way, say, John Adams recalls Sigismundo Malatesta in Pound's *Cantos*. Again a bird, here a gull, signals the presence of the devouring-mother aspect of the feminine, Hecate, and the poet's rendition of the gull's cry, "I. I. I. . . . harsh/in sadness, on and on,/beak and gullet open against the blue," is a complex projection, like much else concerning the female in the poem. Against the speaker's frustrated speechlessness ("I am opening it, / tongue-tied") rings the banal chatter of the guide: "Such a depth of charm / here always . . ." and "with a wicked wit, but self-mocking; / and full of integrity behind it all." Somehow she gets involved in the threat to the poet's own integrity, as she also gets involved in the poet's sense of the gulls as Hecate's birds:

> (and they are on it in a flash,
> brief tongues of movement
> ravenous, burrowing and feeding,
> invisible in blind savagery,
> upstreaming through the sunlight with it
> until it disappears, buried
> in heaven, faint, far off)
>
> (*NLD*, 44)

Tongues, ravenous, feeding, burrowing, the enclosures of George Moore's rooms—we have seen such images and concepts before, and they underscore the irony of the speaker's projection of savagery onto the gulls after his own murderous fantasy. That the fantasy is a far cry from the mood of the speaker in "Phoenix Park" is an obvious enough observation and suggests that the speaker here has more unfinished business with the feminine than finished. In Jungian imagery it is not uncommon to see the anima as a deadly threat, and it is a theory not peculiar to Jung that marauders against women are attacking what they project as all-powerful controlling or disabling figures. What we have in this poem, I think, is a flash of the misplaced rage that is the individual's version of the unassimilated violence of history: maleness, to adopt one terminology, striking out against a repressed sense of weakness imaged as the feminine.

The development toward which all these poems point is fairly candidly asserted in the primary symbol Kinsella assigns to the collection at the end of "hesitate, cease to exist, glitter again," the figure of the egg, the zero. This figure, he has said, rather strikingly omitting any reference to the conventional feminine implications of the symbol,

> is one of the aspects of *Notes*. If the book has a definite numeral, zero is it. It's nothing, it's a hole, it's the opening "from which," and so on. That's why a great deal of the matter in *Notes* swims about with no

apparent control, because in fact it's in this cauldron, this stew of potentiality and raw material. And I think this is psychologically accurate also,
representing the gathering attitude of a young boy's observing mind.
There is not imposition of order, but openness. The "O" is wide open,
and everything is for later consideration. (O'Hara 1981, 17)

The young boy's observing mind makes one last appearance in "The
Liffey Hill." This poem and "Good Night," which follows it to close *Notes
from the Land of the Dead,* constitute the most powerful juxtaposition in
the book. Like the other "daylight" poems in the book—"Tear," "Ancestor," "At the Crossroads," and the others—"The Liffey Hill" serves to
reestablish the conscious-world experiences that are underpinned (or un-
dermined) by the mysterious goings-on of poems like "All Is Emptiness
and I Must Spin." In this poem, however, Kinsella accomplishes the *tour
de force* of composing a splendidly expressive language that almost succeeds in not expressing. It modulates into the recall of a boyhood Christ-
mas morning and concludes,

> Snow powdery pure
> on the wool glove, detailed and soft.
> The day lengthened, and the wool got dark and wet
> and smelled of cold.
> > Flatsour? Raw . . . notsour
>
> Morning, the magical-bright first print, gone . . .
> The air grew dark, and harder.
> We are out too late.
> Voices, far away, die in the cold.
> But there is still the pleasure of going home,
> and dusk closing in, and a good fire.
>
> I scrambled on top of the wall in the lamp-light,
> bundled up in scarf and coat,
> and hugged the iron post, and slipped down.
> My boots scuffled on the path,
> echoing, alone,
> > down the Lane.
> > > (*NLD,* 46–47)

For all its attractiveness, this experience is like that in "Tear," where the
boy cannot *make* anything of what he is describing. Again the clue is the
banal language of the everyday: "But there is still the pleasure of going
home, / and dusk closing in, and a good fire." This is a sensibility chiefly

ensconced in unexamined contact with the physically given, and though he is dimly aware of a resonance of some kind, the speaker was then not one to dwell on resonances: "My boots scuffled on the path, / echoing, alone, / down the Lane." There is a sweet boyishness here, keeping the mind on the more or less superficial business at hand—as the unseen poet may or may not be aware.

On the other hand, a subrational darkness is rehabilitated in the punning title of "Good Night," which ends the third section of *Notes from the Land of the Dead*. We witness there a coming-into-being less ambiguous than that in "All Is Emptiness and I Must Spin" as consciousness dissolves into sleep in what we might well regard as a Kinsellan fusion of Joyce and Jung. The uttering consciousness (we cannot call it the speaker) drifts off to sleep hearing snatches of speech or conversation from a radio in the next room and wanders in and out of dream visions:

> if you look closely
> you can see the tender undermost
> muscle actually forming
> from the rock, and the living veins
> continuing inward, just visible . . .
> (*NLD*, 49)

Interwoven with such strands of semiconscious vision, the overheard conversation marches on

> . . . would you agree, then, we won't
> find truths, or any certainties . . .

contrapuntally to the discoveries of the irrational:

> where monsters lift soft
> self-conscious voices, and feed us
> and feed in us, and coil
> and uncoil in our substance,
> so that in that they are there
> we cannot know them, and that,
> daylit, we are the monsters of our night,
> and somewhere the monsters of our night are . . .
> here . . . in daylight that our nightnothing
> feeds in and feeds, wandering
> out of the cavern. . . .
> (*NLD*, 50)

The imagery here, the mere statements, attest the increasing connectedness of the self as Kinsella has come to view it. They project a consciousness not disabled or terrified by its discoveries of the irrational or the
not-me. The "monsters of our night" which we are and which are yet not
us, the nightnothing that feeds and is fed—these are reflections, I think,
of Kinsella's growing concern to see the urgings of self extended into
contact with the eternal processes of the suprapersonal universe. In this
light, the last words are reclamative entirely: "and ungulfs a Good Night,
smiling"—a drowsy reference to the departing guest-talker, whose conventional phrase of nocturnal farewell speaks more profoundly than he
knows.

Dillon Johnston has remarked on the price Kinsella has paid in shrink-
ing readership for the way of proceeding that I have attempted to elucidate
here (Johnston 1985, 97), yet it is hard to know what alternative the poet
might have had. Quite apart from any poet's absolute right to write what
he must, to eliminate the material from Irish myth or to load the poems
with a string of helpful footnotes would throw Kinsella's work back into
the confines of the conventional lyric—a condition that has in fact impoverished the contemporary poetry of England (but which American and
Irish contemporaries, at least, seem to have avoided so far). As Johnston
reminds us, Yeats "reduces his readers' ignorance with his titles" and with
notes. That Kinsella does not do so is owing, I think, to another Jungian
principle, a major concomitant of the technique of amplification, namely
the principle of *directedness* or *purposiveness*.

In Jacobi's version of Freudian methodology, "Freud asks with his
reduction, 'Why?'; Jung asks in dream interpretation above all, 'To what
purpose?' " For Jung, "The free associations to the unconscious product
are . . . evaluated with respect to where their goal lies and not with respect
to their origin,"[14] for causality is seen as a reductive concept that pursues
interpretative evidence "backward through a chain of free associations
until they, entrapped in causal connections, lead to the *one* point X from
which they proceeded"—not forward, that is, toward a point from which
the psyche can go on, but "back into the complex." No doubt few psycho-
therapists today, however Freudian, really follow so rigid a strategy, but
what is important is the bearing of all this on Kinsella's poetry. The
method oriented to causality is almost a parody of the naïve mimesis such
as inexperienced readers will pursue in attempting to "uncover" what the
poet "was trying to say." Jung's purposive orientation asks rather to what
end behavior is directed, and the answer can almost never be simple:

14. Jacobi 1951, 133–34.

Of course, if we . . . impute rational intentions to the unconscious, the thing becomes absurd. But it would never do to foist our conscious psychology upon the unconscious. Its mentality is an instinctive one; it has no differentiated functions, and it does not 'think' as we understand 'thinking.' It simply creates an image that answers to the conscious situation. This image contains as much thought as feeling, and is anything rather than a product of rationalistic reflection. Such an image would be better described as an artistic vision. (Jung 1966, 192)

Like "Good Night," then, the collection as a whole "ungulfs" a darkness that may turn out to be benign—to be the frightening but restorative exposition of orderable and productive forces, forces that if not oppressed by a defensive consciousness will not hurt and may nurture. Attempting to "let the dawning of individuation control what will happen" is more than a dramatic convention in these poems; supporting it is the emphatically positive aspect of Jungian thought joined with expressive strategies developed through a perceptive reading of Pound, Williams, and Joyce—a complex that helps form the technical and spiritual core of Kinsella's next collection, the astonishing and compendious *Peppercanister Poems 1972–1978*.

5   Human Power
Language, Self, and History

With the publication of *Peppercanister Poems 1972–1978* a remarkable and courageous literary venture comes to fruition, and in part to an end. The three poems of departure that close *Nightwalker* memorialized a departure from Dublin but also from the kind of poetry that preceded them, poetry that had won a great measure of fame and success for Thomas Kinsella. The work that followed marked his embarkation on what would amount to fifteen years of deliberate imaginative research into the nature of his art and its resources. It was an inward turning in both a Jungian and a Poundian sense as Kinsella sought a workable sense of the poetic self and a more potentiating conception of poetic language, with all the questions both of those terms imply: continuity or discontinuity between self and the circumambient world; continuity or discontinuity between language and the world it "handles"; and continuity or discontinuity between the human spirit and the world in which it finds itself. What could perhaps be taken as narrowly programmatic—the clearly deliberate focus on the feminine in the earlier book, for example, with its Jungian machinery and the clearly deliberate progression to a focus on the masculine in *Peppercanister Poems 1972–1978*—is better seen as a dramatic structure, though there is no need to deny what I have characterized as the research aspect of the poetry.

The work in *Peppercanister Poems 1972–1978* both continues and departs from the exploratory building of self that has been the focus of the preceding comments on *Notes from the Land of the Dead*. *Notes from the Land of the Dead* meditates the self for the self's sake. When the self is found connected to historical or cultural templates, as in "Survivor," the lines of force run toward self, which is thus revealed as a fuller entity than daytime life suspects. In *Peppercanister Poems 1972–1978* these connections or ramifications of self are pursued, but here the lines of force run in both directions—the four long poems placed at the beginning of the book all concern powerful public men whose behavior has public effects (this is true even of Seán O'Riada, who, as composer and as founder of the Chieftains, may have left a more enduring mark on history than Lord Widgery or John F. Kennedy). At the same time, the companion preoccupations of self and language approach fusion, and it becomes pointless to continue compartmentalizing the two topics.

The opening focus of *Peppercanister Poems 1972–1978* is on a public man falsely claiming that something terrible didn't happen; the book ends on the figure of a private man acknowledging that something did. Where *Notes from the Land of the Dead* brooded upon experiences undergone, *Peppercanister Poems* in the end turns to language, as it moves from a youthful figure who indeed *undergoes* experience and whose revelations are almost incidental to his accounts of what the experiences felt like, to the figure of a language user whose aim is clarity, articulation, understanding. Almost from its first page the book is a struggle toward a true speech truly aligned with states of affairs.

Given the important principle of composed book in *Notes from the Land of the Dead* and the fact that the vitality of most of the poems in that collection is in part a function of inter-relation, *Peppercanister Poems* can seem more of a departure than it really is, constructed as it is of long poems and sequences, in chronological order, composed over the better part of a decade and apparently centering on a variety of themes and occasions. The first poem in the book, "Butcher's Dozen," is a satiric commentary on the Widgery Report concerning the murder of the Derry civil rights marchers in January of 1972, whereas the sequence *One* that follows returns to the concerns of *Notes from the Land of the Dead* and "Phoenix Park." The two poems on Seán O'Riada seem to sort ill with the assertive public stance of "Butcher's Dozen," and none of the three might seem at first to have much to do with the long meditation on the poet's father in *The Messenger*. The collection looks like what the author's preface more or less says it is, a gathering of eight Peppercanister publications—the Peppercanister series being a publication venture run from Kinsella's home. But the Peppercanister series was a way of placing work in progress, or perhaps the progress of ongoing work, before the public until larger projects were ready. And well before *Peppercanister Poems 1972–1978* was finally assembled, Kinsella was clear on what he wanted it to do. Aware of the seeming tentativity of some of the moves in *Notes from the Land of the Dead* and the poetry that followed, he was aiming among other things to incorporate the material from Irish myth into the poetry "in a dramatic way, almost certainly by having the undefined consciousness, which is at the root of the poems in *Notes*, becoming more defined . . . so that the thing will have a dramatic effect and gather up the mythical Irish contents of the subconscious" (O'Hara 1981, 7). More than "mythical Irish contents" swam into the poet's ken for this collection. If "Old Harry" in *Downstream* was Kinsella's first freewheeling lunge into the material of politics, "Nightwalker," no less outspoken, seems to have been in effect his farewell to such poetry, to an impulse not to be revived until the Derry outrage in 1972. But a pervasive political consciousness is at work all the same in *Peppercanister Poems 1972–1978*, and not only in "Butcher's Dozen." The difference from Kinsella's earlier political poems lies in the point of entry of the political. In the poems under discussion here, politics comes in by the route of mythical, personal, or familial issues, always already knitted up with the experiential reality in which the poet-speaker finds himself.[1] Drawing with ever greater assurance on the structural and epistemological insights he appropriated from the predecessors discussed in the previous chapter, Kinsella weaves a complex web of the historical, the mythical, and the personal, the external and the internal, self and surroundings.

There is a coherence in the move from the shattering of humane ethics in the Derry shootings and Lord Widgery's super-serviceable whitewash through the highly ambivalent privacy of the O'Riada poems, the searching uncertainty of *The Good Fight* ("A poem for the tenth anniversary of the death of John F. Kennedy"), the frank inward turning of the sequence *One*, and the more conventional-seeming poems toward the end of the volume. It is as if the governing consciousness were shocked out of the special form of self-orientation of *Notes from the Land of the Dead* by the brutal onslaught of public events. The Widgery report and the outrage it attempted to explain away[2] constitute the betrayal of an array of major

---

1. Thus McCormack (1987) posits those two concepts as polar in Kinsella's aesthetic only to collapse the distinction as inapplicable—or rather, since he is concerned to disassociate Kinsella from those who would collapse community into politics, he collapses politics into community. If we take "community" to mean all the bearings of cultural surroundings upon self—family, the local and the national past, formal education, and so on—the result is the seamless web of forces manifested in *Peppercanister Poems 1972–1978*.

2. Like the magistrate in Stanley Holloway's comic monologue, "Albert and the Lion," the report that went out over Lord Widgery's name opined that no one was really to blame. The International League for the Rights of Man condemned the Widgery Tribunal Report as an evasive whitewash. See *Justice Denied; A Challenge to Lord Widgery's Report on "Bloody Sunday"* (Defence and Educational Fund 1973).

values, among them a standard of human decency and the value of public speech. Disoriented by the shock of these deaths and the authorities' corrupt evasion of truth, the governing consciousness of the book is, as it were, driven to consider the significance of the lately dead public figure, artist, and private friend, Seán O'Riada, and then to canvass the possible meaning of the ambiguous career of Kennedy. Moving deeper into the mystery of the relation between individual humanity and public signifi- cance, the poems of *One* canvass again, but in an altered mode, the materi- als of Irish prehistory, the family history of the poet himself, and the particular ambience of his youth. The sometimes gruesome *Technical Sup- plement* broods over the prerational underpinnings of civilized life, and the poet reemerges into conscious-world experience in *Song of the Night* and *The Messenger,* the creative journey having brought him toward the human goal proposed in Jacobi's account of Jung: liberation from isola- tion and confusion and into "a wholeness that . . . binds [one's] light, conscious side to the dark one of the unconscious" and makes it possible for one "to find his place in the great stream of life" (Jacobi 1943, 65)— the goal, in Jung's own words, of finding a meaning "which will make possible the very continuation of life, in so far as it is to be more than mere resignation and mournful retrospection."[3]

Like *Notes from the Land of the Dead,* this book has its programmatic emblem, in the title of the major grouping *One.* If the conventionally feminine *O* in *Notes from the Land of the Dead* is "nothing, it's a hole, it's the opening 'from which,' " so that "a great deal of the matter in *Notes* swims about with no apparent control" (O'Hara 1981, 17), the (also conventionally) masculine *One* was "a matter of finding . . . that the poems can organize their own behavior."

> That's why the device for the volume is a snake: a unitary living thing. . . . It is an organizing thing, in Amargin's spine, when he steps onto land for the first time. . . . And "Finistère" is built on the same thing. . . . The "maggot of the possible" wriggling "out of the spine into the brain" —carries the same idea: the zero uncoiling and striking up. . . . Finally, that's why the block of wood in "His Father's Hands" . . . turns into a

---

3. Jacobi 1951, 136. It is important to bear in mind here that neither Jung, probably, nor Kinsella, definitely, has in mind the hygiene of the self pure and simple. For Kinsella, at any rate, the concept of a self that is somehow continuous with some kind of All is not pursued for the aggrandizement of the random ego. Kinsella's poetic self is not in the end a Wordsworthian one nor, for that matter, a self like Whitman's ("I am large; I contain multitudes"), more or less transcending all and pronouncing upon it. Kinsella's self, as I hope has been made clear earlier, is a consciousness *within.* Like the Jungian self at its most developed, it is a part, not a repository for the Most.

great numeral: is struck, and yields all those little squirming potentials.
(O'Hara 1981, 17–18)

The change in emblem signals of course a change from an emphasis
on the womb-like to an emphasis on the phallic. The developing boy of
Notes from the Land of the Dead takes up a masculine principle; enterings
become penetrations, and the exploration of sexuality becomes more complex. The focus moves from the grandmother, whom the poet-speaker in
"Tear" is unable to acknowledge, to put away or kiss good-bye, ultimately
to the father, whose place he eventually takes in an acknowledgment of
the continuity of life. On the way to being more nearly conclusive than
the more exploratory *Notes from the Land of the Dead* (where Kinsella was
"trying to plunge into the land of the dead to find my own roots" [O'Hara
1981, 16]), *Peppercanister Poems* has as its end the realization of the creative self whose founding is initiated in the earlier book.

But there is no fundamental change in method. The method remains
the principle of manifold potentiality. The male principle itself is multiva-
lent, and the very structure of the book turns on working out the shifting
valences of the fact of death. These poems, too, constitute a network of
recurrent images and concerns, deployed and explored in a roughly Poundian way: the issue of beginnings; a preoccupation with images of enterings
very different from those of *Notes from the Land of the Dead,* with images
of water, with odd manifestations of the act of dividing or splitting as
various daylight experiences split open into their psychic content; and
with a pervasive phallic imagery.

The beginnings are cultural, familial, personal, and biological. The
communal migration of "Finistère" and "The Oldest Place" is isomorphic
with the family genesis recounted to young Thomas in "His Father's
Hands"—the legendary ground that incorporates the family into history
and history into the family; in its aspect as an exploratory move, an undertaking, it associates with the poet's launching into verse, his exploration
of his and his people's beginnings, both uniting the poet to his predecessors and validating the poetic act in historical terms. The speaker himself
makes the connection in "His Father's Hands." Musing on family history,
he recurs to ancient communal experience:

> Littered uplands. Dense grass. Rocks everywhere,
> Wet underneath, retaining memory of the long cold.
> (*PcP,* 69)

and his thoughts modulate into meditation on a spirit at once familial and
cultural:

> Dispersals or migrations.
> Through what evolutions or accidents
> toward that peace and patience
> by the fireside, that blocked gentleness . . .
>   (*PcP*, 70)

What he is recalling is not merely an Ireland subject to the tender mercies of English oppression or the holocaust of the Famine, but legendary Ireland as well—specifically, the arrival of the Sons of Mil, the one successful "taking" that, according to legend, finally established the land of Ireland:[4]

> We approached the shore. Once more.
>   Repeated memory
> shifted among the green-necked confused waves.
> The sea wind and spray tugged and refreshed us,
> but the stale reminder of our sin still clung.
>
> We would need to dislodge
> the flesh itself, to dislodge that
> —shrivel back to the first drop
> and be spat back shivering into
> the dark beyond our first father.
>   ("The Oldest Place," *PcP*, 60)

Besides gathering up some of the imagery of *Notes from the Land of the Dead* and seeing the experiences of this and Kinsella's previous volume as anticipated by the antiquity in his very genes, all this imparts significant resonance to such experiences as that in the tenth poem of *A Technical Supplement*, which turns on a new beginning for an old house:

> What an expanse of neglect
> stretched before us!
> Strip to the singlet and prepare,
> fix the work with a steady eye,
> begin: scraping and scraping
> down to the wood,
> making it good, treating it . . .

---

4. In the two poems dealing with the Milesians in *Peppercanister Poems,* and specifically in the song of Amargin in "Finistère," Kinsella is drawing on Part 5 of *Lebor Gabála Erenn* (Macalister 1956).

Growing unmethodical after a while,
letting the thing stain and stay unfinished.
                    (*PcP*, 85)

This threatens to parallel the pain- and disease-marred beginnings in "The Oldest Place" and "Finistère," but the speaker sets to with renewed resolve, depicting the very purpose of the imaginative process that is this book:

> We have to dig down;
> sieve, scour and roughen;
> make it all fertile and vigorous
> —get the fresh rain down!

In *Notes from the Land of the Dead* enterings or penetrations tend to be into places that, when not null like the "Robbers' Den" or the scullery, are full of threats of ingestion and obliteration—the Other as Sheela-na-gig—and little develops once entrance is made. In this collection, on the other hand, we have a whole spectrum of enterings and penetrations, from the destructive and cruel to the creative and fecundating. The migration of "Finistère" is an entering ("We entered into a deep bay") of some significance for the poet and his community. The grandfather's awl in *The Messenger* "pierces the last hole in a sole" and is echoed by, as it echoes, these slashing knives wielded at the slaughterhouse of Swift and Company:

> Three negroes stood on a raised bench before them.
> One knifed the belly open upward to the tail
> until the knife and his hands disappeared
> in the fleshy vulva and broke some bone
>   (*PcP*, 82)

which in turn reproduce the apparently murderous knives of poems *iv* and *v* of *Technical Supplement*. The knives in those two short poems that image in cruel detail just how knives do penetrate flesh are, after all, like the little cobbler's nails driven into the grandfather's work table, and all these associate with the "penetrating senses" of poem *xvi*. "Going in," that is, can be any going in, surgical, sexual, navigational, agricultural—creative, destructive, even casual.

Obviously the sexual is never far off when such imagery occurs, and many of the enterings are, not surprisingly, colored by the pervasive consciousness of the phallic that characterizes the poems. The migrants of "Finistère" are worshipers of great ithyphallic monuments whose building is a fusion of the cultural, the devotional, and the sexual. The poet-hero Amargin prays to the "mild mother" in "whose yearning shadow / we erect our great uprights" (*PcP*, 57). The knife itself of the fourth poem of *Technical Supplement* is phallic:

> Persist.
>   Beyond a certain depth
> it stands upright by itself
> and quivers with a borrowed life.

In a gentler context:

> The pen writhed. It moved
> under my thumb!
>   It has sensed
> that sad prowler on our landing again.
>
> If she dares come nearer, if she dares . . .
> She and her "sudden and
> peremptory incursions" . . .
> I'll pierce her like
> a soft fruit, a soft big seed!
>   (*PcP*, 89)

The moral and emotional potentiality of associational clusters of this sort is of course one of the major issues in the book. If the knife shape, or the shape of the numeral 1, is "the first stroke of order, the zero uncoiling and striking up," it seems that not every stage in this queer uncoiling is necessarily attractive. *One* (1) has the shape of nails, approximately the shape of an explorer's ship, and roughly the shape of the slugs that killed the civil rights marchers who speak in "Butcher's Dozen" and of the weapons that fired them. It is the figurative shape of the motivating impulse that moves Amargin and his fellows in "Finistère" to undertake the voyage to Ireland—the shape of something as trite and as crucial as "backbone" and something as private to the speaker as his grandfather's workbench, a long block of wood which, found one day at the back of the yard, "broke open, / countless little nails / squirming and dropping out of it" (*PcP*, 71)—Kinsella's humorous version of the ithyphallic dream in the first chapter of Jung's *Memories, Dreams, Reflections*. The phallic shape is indeed the shape of many things, and penetration can be the act of fecundation, or it can be detached rifle bullets tearing into human flesh, or, as we have seen, a knife slashing into the body of a defenseless animal whose "processing" we tend not to discuss over dinner, or an idea penetrating a mind.

The preoccupation with this sort of imagery and with penetrations and enterings is not a crude rejection of femininity as such in favor of the masculine as such (though it obviously does constitute a move from the gallery of feminine figures laden with a mysterious power that it is beyond the abilities of the youthful figure in *Notes from the Land of the Dead* to articulate): the speaker is not a Freudian little boy settling his mere sexual destiny. Here the whole machinery of male-oriented sexuality works intimately with the poems' series of significant male personages to form an inclusive awareness of the male consciousness in all its potentialities, from sterile willfulness to creative, loving desire. It may be, to be sure, that the way to the latter is through a Beckettian gloom with respect to the former. In any case, major masculine figures in the poems are deployed throughout a universe of such actions, a universe consistently polyvalent.[5]

Some of the males are precursive figures whose energies are to be assimilated into a productive new personality that will be the poet's, others cautionary *exempla,* drawn perhaps with the thought in mind of the Jungian principle that a productive function can lose its real power by coming adrift from the interactive net of energies that are its proper universe. The slaughterers at Swift and Co.—"Two elderly men in aprons," among others—are wielders of a not unuseful destructive energy, operating, according to their imagery, with a weird eroticism divorced from eroticism's usual concomitants (as, for example, the knife and hands that "disappeared in the fleshy vulva"). They are all male, and as killers they are analogous to the paratroopers in "Butcher's Dozen," though they kill in service to a different principle, and their brutality reveals the gruesome underside of many a good civilized dinner. What principle is served by the killings perpetrated by the British soldiers?

Mr. Cummins, in "38 Phoenix Street," on the other hand, is a pale, horror-haunted version of Amargin; Mr. Cummins, too, has been "Sealed in his sad cave," the prison of his broken self. This disabled Orpheus, explorer of an underworld he never sought, "was buried for three days under a hill of dead, / the faces congested down all around him / grinning

---

5. As polyvalent, it is only fair to add, as the feminine figures in *Notes from the Land of the Dead.* Read one book or one poem at a time, Kinsella can seem almost arrogantly male oriented—Carol Tattersall's diatribe in the *Canadian Journal of Irish Studies* (Tattersall 1990) is a kind of parody of what Kinsella is exposed to. But the female figures in *Notes from the Land of the Dead* have no less "public" pertinence than the masculine figures in *One* and elsewhere.

Dardanelles! in the dark" (*PcP*, 65). The digging down here to get the fresh rain down was accidental: someone happened to notice his "corpse" bleeding. Now, "always hunched down sad and still beside the stove with his face turned away toward the bars," all he has brought from his grisly resurrection is the unassimilated dark in which he was nearly buried.

Amargin is of course a more fruitful figure. He has a distinctive public name and is a component of Irish history and tradition as poet, explorer, judge, leader, penetrator of the promising feminine quantity of ancient Ireland, and, in "Finistère," speaker of the words that sanctify the possession of the land of Ireland by the Sons of Mil (reconciling, in fact, the feminine divinities of the island, Banba/Fotla/Eriu to the act of possession the sons of Mil have come to carry out.)[6] Both as a poet and as a figure of legend, he is a man of words in two senses, and as the latter he is at once firmly in history and yet outside of time—which last, however, will limit his overall usefulness to the poet. Mr. Cummins has been in time, with a vengeance, and has not truly survived.

The poet's grandfather and father, for their part, have been productively in and out of the temporal world on many levels. The grandfather is preeminently a doer—cobbler and barge captain, and presiding figure in a poem pointedly called "His Father's Hands," presiding more particularly over that phallic workbench. And he is clearly a vessel for the transmission of potentialities and a participant in the accretion of meaning around the concept of the male principle—as in the images at once phallic and familial that describe him in "His Father's Hands":

> The blood advancing
> —gorging vessel after vessel—
> and altering in them
> one by one.
>
> Behold, that gentleness already
> modulated twice, in others:
> to earnestness and iteration;
> to an offhandedness, repressing various impulses.
>
> (*PcP*, 70)

In *The Messenger* Kinsella *père* takes up both action and words— words tied to action, political words aimed at ordering the world: at his father's (the speaker's grandfather's) bench, he knows that

---

6. See Macalister 1956, 35–37 and poems 68–70 in the same volume, 111–115.

He will not stick at this . . . The knife blades,
the hammers and pincers, the rasps and punches,
the sprigs in their wooden pits,

. . . .
He reaches for a hammer,
his jaw jutting as best it can
with Marx, Engels, Larkin

howling with upstretched arms into the teeth
of Martin Murphy[7] and the Church
. . . .
Son and father, upright, right arm raised.
Stretching a thread.
Trying to strike right.

(*PcP*, 131, 132)

As this book moves toward its close, the father becomes the most nearly
compendious male figure of the book. He is master of actions public and
private, as union organizer, father, and son, and of speech public and
private, orating in an election campaign at one point, "shouting about the
Blueshirts," and elsewhere (in "His Father's Hands") talking to young
Thomas about the history of his family. Unambiguously engaged in adult
sexuality ("They have tussled in love. / They are hidden, near the river
bank . . . a woman and her secret husband. . . . The body, a glass worm, /
is pulsing. The tail tip winces and quivers: / I *think* this is where I come
in" [*PcP*, 129]), he is also regarded near the beginning of this elegy in
feminine terms—at least as follows:

[I] have watched my hand reach in under
after something, and felt it
close upon it and ease him of it.

The eggseed Goodness
that is also called
Decency.

(*PcP*, 126)

And the poem begins with the assertion that "His mother's image settled
on him / out of the dark, at the last, and the Self sagged, unmanned"—

7. [William] Martin Murphy was the Dublin tycoon, owner of (among other things)
the Dublin United Tramways Company and the newspaper *Independent*, and architect of the
strategy of massive lockouts that broke the back of the industrial action by Dublin's labor
unions under James Larkin in 1913. See Lyons 1973, 282–84.

another manifestation of the insistent doubleness that marks much of this collection.

The deafness that came upon him as upon his own father is factual but also symbolic, in both cases emblematizing the power of selective resistance to the welter of miscellaneous fact with which the outer world bombards us. Yet this cheery reading of the deafness will not finally do. That uneasiness over the modulation of the grandfather's gentleness into "earnestness and iteration; / . . . an offhandedness, repressing various impulses" is connected with it, and the implications surface in an openly Jungian section of *The Messenger*, where the tone, despite the figurative speech, is decidedly clinical:

> Typically, there is a turning away.
> The Self is islanded in fog.
> It is meagre and plagued with wants
>
> but secure. Every positive matter
> that might endanger—but also enrich—
> is banished. The banished matter
>
> (a cyst, in effect, of the subject's aspirations
> painful with his many disappointments)
> absorbs into the psyche, where it sleeps.
>
> Intermittently, when disturbed, it wakes
> as a guardian—or "patron"—monster
> with characteristic conflicting emotional claims:
>
> appalling, appealing; exacting sympathy
> even as it threatens. (Our verb "to haunt"
> preserves the ambiguity exactly.)
>
> Somewhere on the island, Cannibal
> lifts his halved head and bellows
> with incompleteness. . . Or better—
>
> a dragon slashes its lizard wings uneasily
> as it looks out and smells the fog
> and itches and hungers in filth and fire.
>
> (*PcP,* 124)

Viewed in one light, this is the exclusion, the refusal to assimilate, that in Jungian theory is the source of neurosis and derangement. A sleeping animal, it occasionally rouses and "Often . . . the beast was suddenly there / insinuating between us" (*PcP*, 124). Whatever failings in the father prompt that observation, it grows out of a sense of limit imposed, from within and without, by the father's own stubbornness:

> Thumbs in belt, back and forth
> in stiff boots he rocked with the news
> (I care) (But accept) (I reject) (I do not)
>   (*PcP*, 122)

and by circumstances:

> For there is really nothing to be done.
> There is an urge, and it is valuable,
> but it is of no avail.

So, in the poem at least, the father takes to pure action, walking a beam in a brewery where he works and daring "with outstretched arms / what might befall."

> And it befell, that summer,
> . . . .
> that his bronchi wrecked him with coughs
> and the muffled inner
> heartstopping little
> hammerblows began.
>   (*PcP*, 123)

But the poet's words make clear what reading in Jung himself would confirm, that the monster is a Janus figure—not mere "Cannibal," but guardian dragon or, more pertinently, repository of powerful psychic material that, as one commentator has put it, "fuels the poetic project" (O'Hara 1983, 78). For though "*Often, much too familiar for comfort, / the beast was . . . there . . . between us,*" (*PcP*, 124) the cyst which it is becomes first nutritive, "The eggseed Goodness," and then precious: "Goodness is where you find it. / Abnormal. / A pearl. . . . Look in it." (*PcP*, 126–127) "Looking in it" is what the poet in fact does in *The Messenger* itself and in *Technical Supplement*—as in all those poems of his, here and earlier, that seem so drenched in violence. It is a central principle for Jung, as for this poet, that there are no idle wheels in the psyche, that the way to account for impulses is to discover what they are *for*. The monster that bursts forth in savagery when repressed or denied is the wellspring of creative acts and

relations when confronted. The source of the savagery is not the monster
but the denial.

What seems gratuitous gruesomeness in poem *v* in *Technical Supplement*
is actually a brief overture to some savagery most citizens of the current
world would be loath to see done away with:

> A blade licks out and acts
> with one tongue.
> Jets of blood respond
> in diverse tongues.
>
> And promptly.
> A single sufficient cut
> and the body drops at once.
> No reserve. Inert.
> If you would care to enter this grove of beasts:
>   (*PcP*, 80–81)

The grove is the Swift and Co. slaughterhouse, where the poet's party is
treated to "hot confusion and the scream-rasp of saw" and "huge horned
fruit not quite dead," animals still more or less alive hung up by a hook
through the lower leg—standard procedure in the "meat-processing"
plants that deliver our daily protein. Civilization itself—commerce and
cuisine joined in unholy matrimony—furnishes the poet with a concrete
manifestation of the horrors that have been thrust upon him by his "dark,
unconscious side"—and by history, Bloody Sunday included. The
implications for normal life constitute the resonance of the ninth poem
in the sequence, which finds the speaker before an aquarium tank,
another of those devices we have developed to show the monstrous
safely contained:

> A dark hall. Great green liquid windows
> lit. The Stations of the Depths.
> . . . .
> Two morays craned up their exposed shoulders
> from a cleft, the bird-beaked heads
> peering up at a far off music of slaughter,
> moving with it, thick and stiff.
>   (*PcP*, 84)

The grim parody of the spirit of Diderot in *Technical Supplement* is under-lined by the poet's use of the drawing of the scalpel from the *Encyclopédie* on page 73. That scalpel (reproduced from the cover of the 1976 Pepper-canister edition of *Technical Supplement*) seems innocent enough as it ap-pears (by itself) in *Peppercanister Poems 1972–1978*. Few American readers have seen the Peppercanister edition, which reproduces five others of Diderot's illustrations: a writing hand with pen on the title page; a dou-ble-page illustration of a human eyeball being punctured by a dissecting needle; a meticulous drawing of the vascular system of a severed human neck and head; an utterly matter-of-fact drawing of a man using a brace and bit to bore into a human head; and, near the beginning of the book, a geometrically analyzed line drawing of the Laocoön, blithely indifferent to the agony expressed by the figure.[8] The emotional gap between the content of the drawings and the cool detachment they exude is, of course, enormous. The tension between the hunger of the inquiring or observing or poetizing mind and the moral claims of the material being addressed are a major theme in this and later stages of Kinsella's work. But that the poet is not merely smirking at the naïveté of Enlightenment rationalism is made clear by the epigraph (in both the separate edition of *Technical Supplement* and *Peppercanister Poems 1972–1978*): a passage from one of Diderot's letters to Voltaire. Lamenting the squalid and exhausting labor of combating his political persecutors, Diderot decries the uselessness of the whole enterprise of the *Encyclopédie* ("Is it quite clear that . . . there is much difference between the philosopher and the flute-player?") only to conclude, "That there is more spleen than good sense in all this, I admit —and back to the Encyclopedia I go" (*PcP*, 74). These words from an embattled writer fending off feelings of futility are not without application to a contemporary poet whose critical audience is given to seeing him as having disappeared into hermeticism and Jungian arcana (see n. 13 below).

The letter obviously and intentionally jars with the reductive exacti-tude Kinsella renders, the clear rendition of certain truths in baldest detail in both the poems here and the illustrations. (W. J. McCormack is correct in seeing *A Technical Supplement* as striving "to supplement one ideology of enlightenment by unpeeling or flaying it" [McCormack 1987, 77].) But the source of the quoted letter, a chapter in Viscount Morley's book on Diderot (Morley 1923, 157), is an interesting addition to the context of *Technical Supplement*. For one thing, it describes an eighteenth-century France that resembles the dreary pictures of mid-twentieth-century Ireland

8. See Kinsella 1976.

2. Laocoön (plate xxxvi from the section "Dessein" in Diderot's *Encyclopédie*). "Blitherly indifferent to the agony expressed by the figure." Courtesy of the Department of Special Collections, Van Pelt-Dietrich Library, University of Pennsylvania.

drawn by Terence Brown and F. S. L. Lyons: "As we cannot too clearly realize, it was the flagrant social incompetence of the church which brought what they called Philosophy, that is to say Liberalism, into vogue and power" (Morley 1923, 144); and "The old principle was decrepit [in 1758–59], it was not able to maintain itself; the hounds were furious, but their fury was toothless" (Morley 1923, 154).[9] In the treachery of the bookseller Le Breton, the licensee for the *Encyclopédie* who secretly took to censoring the copy Diderot sent to him, callously cutting out anything that looked like it might arouse the disapproval of Church or government, we can perhaps find an echo of the complicity of the Irish populace in the admittedly milder fastidiousness of the church in Ireland in the decades after independence. In Morley's remarking in the same chapter (p. 183) that the *Encyclopédie* seems like Vergil's *Georgics* to be a glorification of manual labor on the part of this son of a cutler who "might well bring handicraft into honour" there lies a clear parallel with Kinsella and the poem honoring his working-class father.

These possibly incidental trivia point to a subtext having to do with the maturing of some central tendencies in Kinsella's aesthetic. Much of the discussion so far has recurred to terms like "polyvalent," "shifting valences," "resonance" and such, and I have suggested that the "lines of force" that run between entities in this late book exhibit greater complexity than such phenomena did even in *Notes from the Land of the Dead*. The coincidental parallels between Diderot and the speaker-poet of *Peppercanister Poems 1972–1978* and the perhaps equally coincidental parallel of Morley's "France" to Kinsella's "Ireland" are in keeping with the persistent sense of isomorphism elsewhere in Kinsella's work that needs no such apologetic qualification. McCormack's adducing the concept of allegory (above, p. 49) was anticipated by the interview with Haffenden in 1980. When Haffenden raised the issue of "allegorical figures" in *Nightwalker*, Kinsella replied, "The obsession with fact, with specific data, wouldn't seem to me to make much sense unless it had some allegorical drive behind it. Experience by itself, however significant, won't do" (Haffenden 1981, 104). Earlier he had said to Daniel O'Hara,

> that's why the block of wood in "His Father's Hands," which did also exist, turns into a great numeral: is struck, and yields all those little squirming potentials [i.e., the "countless little nails / squirming and drop-

---

9. Morley's tone with respect to the Catholic Church, of course, is the tone of a borderline fanatic on the evils of Catholicism of a sort that can still be found, and I do not wish to imply any agreement with his attitudes on my part.

ping out of it"]. It happened! There seems to be—so far I've been lucky in finding—a simple organizing idea which brings this real matter into proper use. (O'Hara 1981, 18)

For Kinsella, in short, it matters that fact and meaning are in some way substantively continuous. That poetry can use language allegorically is owing to the fact that lines of force can be experienced as existing (and here, interestingly enough, we are in the conceptual world of William Carlos Williams, for whom the forming of comparisons was a practice of little worth in poetry, whose major business is with *connections*). And as it is with fact and value, language and scene, so it is with fact and fact or scene and scene, and the Peppercanister poems build heavily on the isomorphic relations the poet sees between one entity and another: between myth and personal experience, between family and nation, between history and myth—and these isomorphic relations are clearly not to be dismissed as coincidental.

There remains, however, a distinction to be drawn. The scene at the aquarium is "allegorical" in the sense Kinsella and Haffenden seem to give the term in that interview; its language presents a (somewhat) covert analogy between the fish and events in the human world presented elsewhere in the book. But the reference to "Swift's slaughterhouse" in the context of *A Technical Supplement* adheres at once both to the meat processing plant and to an earlier Swift and the Ireland he knew during the time of the composition of, say, *A Modest Proposal*. The passage in *The Messenger* about "The Self . . . islanded in fog" is no less double: "Every positive matter / that might endanger—but also enrich— / is banished" (*PcP*, 124). This banished matter, as we have seen, develops "conflicting emotional claims: / appalling, appealing," until "Somewhere on the island, Cannibal / lifts his halved head and bellows / with incompleteness." Again it is important that the passage ostensibly refers to the poet-speaker and his father: a familial situation, in short, inescapably isomorphic with a cultural or communal prototype—for the "islanded self" here is clearly a version of modern historians' renditions of post-Independence Ireland. The point is not Kinsella's stylistic cleverness but the principles that form his vision of reality. As McCormack points out with respect to passages like these, in Kinsella's work "The political layer is not symbolic of some superior value into which it might be transformed: it is already a structural element of that value" (McCormack 1987, 76)[10]—that is, knitted up, as I

10. In the same place McCormack also makes the point about "the Self" and the term "islanded."

said earlier, with the experiential reality in which the poet finds himself. Overall, the methodology has much to do with why Kinsella (like many a developing modern poet, to be sure) felt constrained to abandon fixed forms and regular metrics after *Downstream*. Conventional poetic form can seem *imposed* on experience; what Kinsella is positing in this later work is a poetry whose shape is a shape shared with existential reality. The shape of the poem is also the shape of an experience, and on this model the poet can claim at the least that his or her language is *congruent* with reality if not a definitive "rendition" of it.

The use of language here is a mark of how far Kinsella had come since *Nightwalker*. With this methodology, if one wishes to call it that, the verbal structures that were chastely ostensive in Kinsella's earliest work and rebelliously suggestive, "resonant," in work like "Phoenix Park" become the "names" not of single things but of classes of things. The isomorphic interrelations among phenomena reveal themselves to the poet and are handed on to an audience in the verbal structures of his work—even, such is the phenomenological order of reality, in the nominative power of single terms like "Swift's slaughterhouse." To decide whether all this should be credited (sentimentally) to the poet's "insight" or (jejunely) to his mere power over words is to court an idle distinction.

It should be added in this connection that the power of the grotesque dispassionateness of Diderot's illustrations clearly left its mark on Kinsella—hence such concrete visual symbols as the Bloody Sunday memorial emblem at the beginning of the book, the eroded portrait of Plato at the head of the Kennedy poem, and the strangely sperm-like drawing by Anne Yeats at the beginning of *One*. Like Kinsella's language, these pictures speak as Diderot's do not. The eroded portrait speaks plainly enough of Kennedy in a compacted way not open to language, and Anne Yeats's drawing, a visual prologue, embodies the union of the feminine *O* and the masculine *1*. True illustrations in a sense in which Diderot's are not, they are visual extensions of the poetry.

It is tempting to see some of these moves of Kinsella's as the manifestation of a pervasive doubleness in his work. Indeed, he invited such an inference in his conversation with Daniel O'Hara, when he said of "Finistère" and "The Oldest Place," "Another false beginning. You're getting the first hint of the division of 'One' into its first two units" (O'Hara 1981, 18). The recurrence of the motif in *Peppercanister Poems 1972–1978* further invites such a reading. If he had continued his numerological procession *through* the number 2 instead of *to* it, one could rest content with the (rather impoverished) concept of doubleness. But what is really involved is something like mitosis, the process of cell division by which organisms develop and grow. Once the single cell splits into two, the way is open to infinite numbers of subsequent cells, and numerology becomes irrelevant: 2 is as far as one need go to launch a potentially endless process. (This may be why Kinsella has subsequently spoken so little of his interest in a series of numbers.) Jung's version of this process of fruitful dividing, which is also involved in the shape of Kinsella's thought here, is that all existence proceeds from the interaction of opposites. The "breakdown," then, of the integrity of *one*, as in the drawing by Anne Yeats, initiates the existence of a productive *two*, which will issue in the infinite multifariousness of reality as we know it. Doubling is but the simplest form of the complicated isomorphism that characterizes Kinsella's imaginative conception of the world.

Vis-à-vis "civilized" society, the material in the slaughterhouse poems and the scene at the aquarium is near kin to the encysted repressed that constitutes the obstructive beast thrusting itself between the poet and his father in *The Messenger*. Transformed there by acceptance into the "eggseed Goodness," it becomes the magical pearl into which the poet gazes to meditate upon stages in the father's life before the blows of illness, the world, and age:

> Goodness is where you find it.
> Abnormal.
>   A pearl.
>
> A milkblue
> blind orb.
>   Look in it:
>
> It is outside the Black Lion, in Inchicore.
> A young man. He is not much more than thirty.
> He is on an election lorry, trying to shout.
>   (*PcP*, 127)

The poet's mind moves back through time to a beginning, the father's first real job, adolescent messenger for the Post Office. On the penultimate page of the poem, Kinsella pays loving and humorous homage both to his father and to the elegy as a form when the father (then still a son, of course) is described as undergoing a droll apotheosis:

He unprops the great Post Office bicycle
from the sewing machine and wheels it through the passage
. . . .
through the shop and into the street.
It faces uphill. The urchin mounts. I see
a flash of pedals! And a clean pair of heels!

(*PcP*, 133)

It is important that the father undergoes this happy metamorphosis
into Hermes specifically as a youth, that the poet has to work his way back
through his parent's history to find that point where, moving out toward
the world, the father was not yet sullied or blocked by the world. As an
actual functioning person, the father does not escape the qualifications to
which every pragmatic manifestation of the male principle is subjected in
this book. To see clearly what bearing all this has on the poet-son, we
must turn first to the other male figures in the collection whose limitations
illuminate the nature of the male principle in its fullness and who figure
importantly in the development of two major themes that have not yet
been discussed: evil and the question of death.

The first four poems in the collection—the *aisling*, or vision-poem,
on the Widgery Report; the two poems on the life and death of Seán
O'Riada, the Irish musician and friend of Thomas Kinsella, and that concerning the assassination of John Kennedy—were written and published
separately a half-decade before *Peppercanister Poems 1972–1978* was assembled. Their inclusion here is pointed and purposeful, not simply a gathering of uncollected work to date. The first and fourth are public poems,
unlike any that follow, and the second and third are about a figure partly
public, partly private. In one way or another, all four are about failed male
figures, about death, and in at least two cases, about evil. In a way, the
poems build a picture of a world whose vital energies have become dys-
functional. So put, this sounds like a world not unfamiliar to readers of
Kinsella's early work, but here there are two pertinent analogies that mark
this version as more intelligibly seen than the glum moral and historical
landscapes of his first collections. One analogy is with Jung's conception
of the complex as the withdrawal of a pyschic faculty or function from its
place in the psychic whole—coming adrift or violating the limits that
mark its healthy position in the functional system as a whole. The other
analogy is to Kinsella's view of the poetic process with respect to the bald
imposition of order—always for Kinsella, as we have seen, a deadening or
distorting violation of actuality. These two political poems bespeak the

sequestering of the political, a significant ordering power broken off from the communitarian whole and, like the uncontrollable neurotic complex in Jung, *imposed* upon a whole to which it is no longer organically related: imposed as brute force and mendacity in the world of "Butcher's Dozen," imposed as (self-?) deceptive rhetoric and political flimflam in "The Good Fight."

This latter poem, completed at some ten years' remove from the enthusiasm for the Kennedy presidency and the excited woe over the assassination, focuses on Kennedy as a man of both words and deeds but takes his words with more than a grain of salt. In fact, all three of the leading voices in the poem are called into question.

> "If other nations falter
> their people still remain what they were.
> But if our country in its call to greatness
> falters, we are little but the scum
> of other lands. That is our special danger,
> our burden and our glory.
> . . . .
> —embrace it!—explosive—to our bodies."
>
> (*PcP*, 39)

Such grandiose rhetorical gestures of Kennedy's as this are subjected to the poet's ironic assessment:

> It sounds as though it could go on forever,
> yet there is a shape to it—Appropriate
> Performance. Another almost perfect
> working model . . .

as well as to the ironic running commentary of Socrates:

> (*Where is a young man's heart in such a scene:*
> *Who would not be stunned by the beast's opinion?*
> *Nor think wisdom control of the beast's moods? . . .*)[11]
>
> (*PcP*, 40)

11. See *The Republic* 494c, Hamilton 1963, 730. These quotations from Plato are the tips of massive allusive icebergs whose function is similar to that of Kinsella's appeal to the *Encyclopedia* and Morley. The sources—book 6 of the *Republic* and various passages in *Laws* —are like Morley's book on Diderot in echoing contemporary situations. Much of the dialogue in *Republic* 6 and in *Laws* has to do with the beleaguered righteous or potentially righteous man (in *Republic 6,* a potential political leader), and both texts are heavy with analogies to poet and politician in twentieth-century society.

The posturings of this spectacular politician (clearly related, it seems to me, to what Kinsella had admired and then rejected in Auden—grace under pressure, "all those superficial things") seem in the end only another version of the self-absorption demonstrated on a humbler scale (he had no invasion of Cuba to authorize) by Lee Harvey Oswald, who speaks a rhetoric of his own:

> I have glided in loveless dream transit
> over the shadowy sea floor,
> satisfied in the knowledge
>
> that if I once slacken in my savagery,
> I will drown.
>
> (*PcP*, 43)

Neither Kennedy's high-flown oratory nor Oswald's narcissistic prose is really aimed at ordering a world; and in the linguistic world inhabited by this poem, the incurably stylish and sanctimonious co-option of Robert Frost as official eulogist yields rhythms and structures dry-rotted and wavering:

> I am in disarray. Maybe if I
> were to fumble through my papers again . . .
> I can no longer, in the face of so much
> —so much . . .
>   It is very hard
>
> (*PcP*, 48)

This is all very sad, and to a certain frame of mind even tragic. It is one of those collapses of rhythm, like the deliberately awkward "repressing various impulses" in that passage from *The Messenger* (above, p. 120) that are Kinsella's characteristic signals of destructive loss of energy—spiritual, ethical, or emotional.[12]

The sense of waste is even stronger in "Vertical Man," whose central figure is both public, as Ireland's leading musician before his death, and

---

12. Compare the adaptation from Queen Victoria's diaries in "Nightwalker" (66):

> There are times it is all a meaningful drama
> Beginning in the grey mists of antiquity
> And reaching through the years to unknown goals
> In the consciousness of man, which is very soothing.

deeply private, as Kinsella's friend and, judging by some parts of the poem, his alter ego. But for all the devotion poured into this poem, it cannot come to terms with the event and personality upon which it focuses. Its mode is again meditative, but it comes to rest repeatedly on remembered events that yield only themselves and their emotional tones. The remembered deathbed visit:

> Gold and still he lay,
> on his secondlast bed. *Dottore!* A withered smile,
> the wry hands lifted. . . .
> . . . .
> *Salut.*
> Slan.
> *Yob tvoyu mat'.*
> Master, your health.
>
> (*PcP*, 26–27)

and the recollected events at the end of the poet's account of a postmortem visit by O'Riada's spirit:

> He stepped forward through the cigarette-smoke
> to his place at the piano
> —all irritation—and tore
> off his long fingernails to play.
> . . . .
> We leaned over the shallows from the boat slip
> and netted the little grey shrimp-ghosts
> snapping, and dropped them
> in the crawling biscuit-tin.
>
> (*PcP*, 33)

These memories are alike in being mainly consolatory: they lead nowhere; they knit the observing mind into the web of implicit bafflement from which the path of understanding that the book follows is a release. In the context furnished by *Notes from the Land of the Dead* the three poems can be seen as presenting defective manifestations of the maleness toward which the speaker develops. Kennedy, all public, is doomed one way or the other. O'Riada is less doomed than wasted (hence the inconclusiveness of the nostalgic images). Partly public and partly personal, he is more like the figure the poet will become than Kennedy is, partly because of the near-continuity of private self and public power he manifests, his art not the manipulative one of political eloquence but the expressive one of music. In *Peppercanister Poems* it will be the destiny of the poet-speaker to fuse all these—eloquence, expressiveness, private self, and public presence.

The issue of evil emerges unambiguously in the bravura performance of "Butcher's Dozen," Kinsella's infuriated *aisling* on the mendacious Widgery Report. The aspect of a failed masculine principle is present here, too, of course, in that the principles are again all male. The Jungian—not "Freudian"—symbolic sexual overtones of the unseen bullets and rifle shapes are given, as has been seen, a strong and persuasive context elsewhere in the book, though as objects they are barely referred to here. Like Kennedy and like Oswald-as-assassin, Widgery and the anonymous paras are all men of power. Now, it is an underlying conviction of this collection that *all* human beings are persons of power, but in a different sense: our power is the power to create, foster, and order life, no matter how complicated or darkly qualified the process may be. The paratroopers merely have the power to do to randomly chosen Irish Catholics what O'Riada, with the help of alcohol, cigarettes, and disease, perhaps did to himself and what Oswald apparently did to Kennedy. But Widgery is the deeper power, and the worse evil, for he is the word-wielder, a version of Kennedy, Frost, and Kinsella whose words are action absolute. And thus early in the book the poet puts his finger on the one source of evil his mode of thought is willing to posit: denial. This—the refusal to acknowledge, to incorporate, to assimilate—is the central Jungian sin, and that is what makes Widgery's evasion wicked in addition to repulsive. He represents a "Law that lets them, caught red-handed,"

> Halt the game and leave it stranded,
> Summon up a sworn inquiry
> And dump their conscience in the diary.
> During which hiatus, should
> Their legal basis vanish, good,
> The thing is rapidly arranged:
> Where's the law that can't be changed?
>   (*PcP*, 15)

And one of the victims says of the British,

> Theirs is the hardest lot to bear,
> Yet not impossible, I swear,
> If England would but clear the air,
> And brood at home on her disgrace
> . . . .

Good men every day inherit
Father's foulness with the spirit,
Purge the filth and do not stir it.
Let them out! At least let in
A breath or two of oxygen,
. . . .
We all are what we are, and that
Is mongrel pure.

(*PcP*, 19)

It is a simpleminded enough observation that events have consequences
and sometimes even meanings that cannot be dealt with unless the event
is at least recognized as having occurred. The way of the Widgerite is the
way of festering and corruption, for it will make no such recognition.

For a poet, of course, assimilation is primarily a matter of words, their
discovery and appropriate deployment, and that is what the rest of the
volume is so much concerned with; it is the record of the unfolding of a
consciousness, and these four more or less public poems stand as cautionary scenes. If entire long poems can be images, these are images of work
not done, of the pitfalls that lie in wait for the unwary ego. Again, isomorphism: "Butcher's Dozen" responds to a brutal version of the denial en-
acted by the father in *The Messenger,* and the ambiguity that invites one to
extend the vision to Ireland itself echoes the remarks of a host of historians
about the puritanical parochialism of the country—a rigid web of denials
that are felt to have impoverished and emasculated the nation, oppressed
and deprived its women, and thinned, or tried to, the watery gruel of its
culture. The images constituted by these poems raise the specter of the
violent death in the midst of which we live, and they pose a set of psychic
investigative challenges that cannot, it seems, be carried on at so public a
level as that even of "The Good Fight." In this series of public or partly
public poems, the Kennedy poem is placed last—a comment on the inadequacy of the pragmatic political—and as the book is set up, the wavering
public voice of the poet as sanctimonious decoration—Frost—is followed
by the intense inward turning of *One.*

I have spoken of the poet's position in all this only in general terms up to
now. He—or a projection of him—is, of course, a presence in the processes his verse reports long before he is a discernible personage. In fact,
though Kinsella uses many experiences from his own actual life, he himself
is not a personage in the usual sense of the word. The nearest analogue to
his poet-speaker would be something between the Dante of the *Commedia*

and the rather spectral narrator of *The Waste Land* or Pound's mercurial narrator in the *Cantos*. (The studied blandness with which Kinsella's passes through the inferno of the slaughterhouse poems in *Technical Supplement* must surely constitute one of the jewels of recent poetry.) This Dantescan figure functions in two ways. In one aspect he is the crucible of consciousness (the cauldron of *Notes from the Land of the Dead*) in which seethe the multifarious, sometimes frightening energies of being to which his anecdotes expose us; in another he is the more or less specific developing consciousness to which I have several times referred. Without ascribing to these two collections of poems a novelistic coherence they do not really have, it is fair to say that the poet who descends into the irrational vision of pre-infancy in the prologue to *Notes from the Land of the Dead* is entering a process that culminates in his emergence from the funeral chapel at the end of *Peppercanister Poems* as a father, like and unlike the one who has died.

Life and his own willing alertness lead him toward the integration desiderated by Jung and by Kinsella's own aesthetic and ethic. Life thrusts upon him the consciousness of sonship, fatherhood, savagery, love, death, desire, serenity. Events, notions, phenomena "crack open," as in the poet-speaker's perception of himself in a distorting mirror in poem *xxii* of *A Technical Supplement* ("It began to separate, the head opening / like a rubbery fan . . . / The thin hair blurred and crept apart . . . as the forehead opened down the center" [*PcP*, 94]), or in poems *xvii* and *xviii*, where casual experiences of eating suddenly dissolve into their cannibalistic historical analogues—one dissolving into productive two. As always in Kinsella's later work, life in its fullness has a large element of the savage, but the point is not that life is ugly. Jung's and Kinsella's idea that the desirable and the terrible, the tender and the murderous, dark and light, are ineluctably interinvolved is an attempt to confront the wholeness that is the only true ground of productive, organic order.

Skeptical about the deaths in the Kennedy affair, enraged by the deaths affronted by Widgery, and baffled—and perhaps not even conscious that he is baffled—by the death of O'Riada, Kinsella is finally brought to the expressive and truly communicative death of his father. This death is an inspiration to meditation and review, an occasion for a passing on of the impulse toward order—moral and political in the father; psychic, moral, and aesthetic in the son. The dyings constitute a continuum of meaning, from heedless murder to a dying that is more than a dying.

Two faculties enable Kinsella's poet figure to penetrate to this level of coherent significance: his openness of consciousness and his particular use of speech. He is the only man of words in these poems whose speech is consistently an act of exploration. The speech of Oswald and Kennedy we have considered already; Amargin is soon transcended: his speech acts are prayers and factual accounts, not pragmatic components in a course of action as Kinsella's are; they serve action but do not fuse with it. The father's language is richer. Unlike Kennedy's political speech acts as Kinsella presents them, the father's words attempt to order life, to bring theory and action into alignment, to join *logos* and *ergon*. But even his political oratory turns on putative givens, the ultimate limitation of all pragmatic discourse. And emerge though he may from the shop into life as the boy messenger, he will emerge from the funeral chapel on the next page to be wheeled to his grave. The figure of the poet, on the other hand, has no données. He speaks to register, to consider, to express, and such themes as he may have develop dialectically from the interactions of the various experiences he presents, not by any mere declaration even only implicit.

This is not rejection, but a development that builds on each preceding step; the father as Messenger becomes the son as Bard—ultimately the son as father, which no man can become without the help of his own parent. And there is one fascinating Jungian aspect left. No more than *Notes from the Land of the Dead* does this collection of poems, no matter how tightly knit we may see it, reach true resolution. Resolution is not an aspect of Kinsella's outlook. What is reached is a point from which life can go on—in this book, the point where the blockage created by performances like the Widgery Report are removed. For interestingly enough, the figure of the narrating poet himself has disappeared altogether in the last part of *The Messenger*. We see the coffin, "the oak box gleaming in the May morning air," and "Our scattered tribe," which "began gathering itself / and trudged off onto a gravel path after it":

> By their own lightness
> four girls and three boys separated themselves
> in a ragged band out from our dull custom
>
> and moved up close after it, in front,
> all shapes and sizes,
> grandchildren, colourful and silent.
>
> (*PcP,* 134)

These are the concluding words of the volume—which is to say that the poet is wielding a language at the service not of an ego, but of a flow of life, and *he* emerges from the funeral chapel not as an assertive self, but as a vision of life going on.

In poetry like this, Kinsella gives up much of what more conventional poets depend upon. Sometimes he gives up syntax, more usually the retailing of facticity—for both of which ventures Kinsella has been criticized by commentators whom we'd expect to know better.[13] Most daring of all, I think, is its giving up the very idea of resolution. It gives up all this to allow something as suspiciously unfashionable as a life-force to move and function on its own terms, for only in this way can an authentic Whole even be glimpsed. Son of a divided country, citizen of a fragmented world, he turns to the depths of the self to envision what transcends that very world. As with Jung in the words of Jolande Jacobi, so with Thomas Kinsella on the evidence of his poetry: "the goal is always totality."

13. Calvin Bedient (*New York Times Book Review,* 16 June 1974, p. 4), for example, saw the poems in *Notes from the Land of the Dead* as for the most part fragments ("The dream poems . . . are conceptually tired," whatever that means), and even Hugh Kenner has said that "Here is one measure of what Kinsella's intensely solipsistic verse cannot accomplish; when he would give us information, even the kind of iconic information around which a personal legend may gather, he knows he must do so in prose" (Kenner 1979, 599).

Afterword

On a rainy Saturday in June, a poet, a scholar/critic, and a young research assistant stood in the downpour before the entrance of Frawley's store in Thomas Street, Dublin, the poet evincing a mixture of courteous patience and nostalgia while the scholar/critic contemplated the purchase of a plastic mac to shield his camera from the rain. Earlier, when we had parked the car in the grim precincts of Swift's Alley (!), the poet pointed out the opening of Molyneux Yard, "a laneway that's been in use since medieval times." He was leading us through the streets—what American journalists call the blue-collar neighborhood—of his childhood and of his poetry: Bow Lane, Kilmainham Lane, Phoenix Street, Thomas Street. The contrast with the serene comfort of the poet's current home in the hills of Wicklow could hardly have been greater. A few yards beyond Frawley's a woman in a ragged sweater and a pair of torn half-gloves stood behind a makeshift stand hawking two packets—two packets!—of pipe tobacco. In phraseology accurate if somewhat remote from the vivid reality of scenes like that, Dillon Johnston has remarked that as a child of grim urban Ireland, Kinsella "developed a wounded sense of the disparity between the real and the ideal world" (Johnston 1985, 74). The culture that produced this Irish poet has been (among other things to be sure) a congeries of such historically intolerable dichotomies—Ireland-Britain, Protestant-Catholic, Republican–Free State, Irish Republic–the Six Counties, and in Kinsella's own family experience, Guiness Corporation–Guiness workers. One might well reflect on the bearing of all this on a mind that found a powerful illumination and a powerful rhetorical tool in the Jungian theory that reality grows out of the conflict and conflation of opposites, its bearing on a poet whose work would flower in contact with the tension-laden juxtapository poetics of Joyce, Pound, and Williams. The man waiting patiently before Frawley's that June Saturday is simultane-

141

ously the son of a Dublin brewery worker and a major figure of his country's literature.

As the poet stood before 38 Phoenix Street jotting down the phone number of the estate agent whose placard advertised the house as for sale, one saw that the silver cord had not been broken. What the poet's feelings were about this visit to his childhood places I do not yet know. But it seemed clearer that day why the transformation of contradiction into dialectic should have become this poet's major preoccupation, and it became vividly clear that one key had been these very sites so laden with contradiction. In a physical ambience like this, with Thomas Kinsella at your elbow, you awaken, if you haven't already, to an intense awareness of how Kinsella's points of reference, in their implicative, weighted nature, answer to the language of his middle and later writing—and vice versa. The polysemous language to which W. J. McCormack pointed is the blood relation of a wrenchingly polyvalent material ground.

The definitive manifestation of the individuated poetic self that concludes *The Messenger*—and thus *Peppercanister Poems 1972–1978*—can fairly be said to mark the successful culmination of the period of Kinsella's courageous researches into his art and into himself as poet. Not that the *art* thus "culminates": the poet who emerges from that period (as he emerges from the chapel at the end of *The Messenger* in what is perhaps a final note from the land of the dead) embodies a powerful congeries of concepts, mindset, and grasp of language that will allow his work to embrace fruitfully any aspect of the world he might confront. The substance of the discoveries, developments, and processes for which I have argued unquestionably marks the work Kinsella has completed since *Peppercanister Poems 1972–1978*. At the time of writing, four Peppercanister sequences along with *The Messenger* have been gathered into the book *Blood and Family* (1988): *Songs of the Psyche* (9), *Her Vertical Smile* (10), *Out of Ireland* (11), and *St. Catherine's Clock* (12). Peppercanister 14 and Peppercanister 15, *Personal Places* and *Poems from Center City*, appeared in 1990, *Madonna* (16) and *Open Court* (17) in 1991—these last published by the Dedalus Press (the death of Liam Miller halted the work of the Dolmen Press). All bear the stamp of the mind and the genius that are embodied in and embody the poetry discussed by this book—address a self, and you find the world; address an aspect of the world, and you find a self. More important, address an aspect of the world and find the rest of the world bearing on the subject of address.

The obverse of that coin is the method that governs a sequence like *St.*

3. The High Road (Kilmainham Road/Bow Lane). "Up the High Road / I held hands, inside on the path, beside the warm / feathery grass."

4. 38 Phoenix Street (with poet). "We knelt on our chairs in the lamp-light . . . watching the gramaphone / The turning record shone and hissed / under the needle, liftfalling, liftfalling."

Catherine's Clock, a lingual fusion of expressive modes—painting, writing, speaking—and a matching interflow of levels of experience—history, personal relationships, family. Pursuing infinite riches in a very little room, the setting of these poems is confined to that small area of west Dublin, just south of Phoenix Park—Francis Street, Thomas Street, Bow Lane—the area of Kinsella's childhood. Relatively late in the poet's life, that is, the poetry returns to sites that figured significantly in earlier work—in *Notes from the Land of the Dead,* for example (particularly the section *"an egg of being"*) and *One.* Like a Kinsellan poem indeed, the locale can be felt to dissolve into its many resonances: Bow Lane, the High Road of the poem in *Notes from the Land of the Dead,* extends at one end to the old Kilmainham Jail, where the British Empire exerted its care for civilization by executing sixteen leaders of the Easter Rising (one of whom was too sick with gangrene to stand up) and at the other to St. Catherine's church, where the Empire hanged Robert Emmet and mutilated his corpse. Portions of the street back on the grounds of Swift's Hospital, and when the young boy of "The High Road" notes how "stony darkness . . . trickled down Cromwell's Quarters, step by step" and feels "A mob of shadows / mill in silence on the Forty Steps," (*NLD,* 16) he may be responding to a local legend that a river of human blood ran down those steps during one of Cromwell's enthusiastic bouts of ethnic cleansing. The scenes in *St. Catherine's Clock* range from such things as a Cruikshank engraving of an episode in Emmet's rebellion of 1803 and a painting of Emmet's brutal execution to a reminiscence of the poet-speaker as a child swatting flies in an upstairs bedroom, happily ignorant of the dimly perceivable analogy between his action and aspects of his neighborhood's history. The clock tower of St. Catherine's in Thomas Street is a material embodiment of the temporal encased in an emblem of the divine and eternal, the magnetic north of the utterances that are the poems in the sequence. To contemplate the building is at once to notice the time of day, look at if not regard a site of religious observance, gaze willy-nilly at the site of a brutal and vindictive execution, and in part to behold the architectural linchpin of a neighborhood and possibly a landmark for one's childhood wanderings. As in Kinsella's work before this, the whole meaning of the building, of the *phrase* that is its name, consists of all these referents and more. The poems in the sequence dissolve the site into its psychic, artistic, political, and personal associations—they do not *trade* on the associations but rather *read* the object itself, bringing into play its entire load of meanings.

Possibly the clearest and perhaps the most powerful manifestation of Kinsella's post-*Messenger* aesthetic is *Her Vertical Smile,* the very epigraph of which fuses the discoursing mind with the mind of another, the room

5. The Forty Steps, leading to Cromwell's Quarters. "(A mob of shadows / mill in silence on the Forty Steps; / ghost-horses back and plunge, turning / under slow swords.)"

in which they used to meet, and the world bodied forth by music: "I remember the elaborate, opulent close of *Der Rosencavalier* filling the mean little space: the unmade single bed, the dusty electric fire glowing in the grate, spattered with butts, Reidy's narrow unfocused face intent in the dark like an animal. I heard Mahler there for the first time" (*VS*, 42). Like *St. Catherine's Clock*, this sequence reaches beyond its own art form, taking the terms *overture, intermezzo,* and *coda* as the titles of its three parts, and taking the overall form, as it seems, of a fantasy of an orchestral performance. Inevitably the "performance" as such dissolves into aspects—the personal bearing of the performance, for example, of the celebrated but unnamed conductor/composer:

> Everything a man can do,
>   and more, is done,
> the sparse hair thrown back,
>
> the white cuffs flaring,
>   the ivory baton flourished
> and driven deep.
>   (*BF*, 44)

No less inevitably, the subject also dissolves—into sexuality in this last passage, but also into warfare and politics as "Overtures and alliances. / White gloves advance, / decorated bellies retire / down mirrored halls. / Entente. Volte face," and "there are great iron entities / afloat like towns erect on the water / with new murderous skills / and there are thunderclouds gathered / on our perimeter, and the Empire / turns once more toward its farrow" (*BF*, 46).

Thereupon the language, ostensibly presenting the fictive conductor/composer, can well be read as gathering up Kinsella's late friend Seán O'Riada (the Reidy of the epigraph) as well:

> And it is his last year, and the last time
>   he is to introduce a new work to us,
> and we can tell.
> . . . .
> Our Music Master . . .

After an interlude focused on the speaker's imagination of Adam and Eve, the poem turns frankly to war—World War I, which furnished us with those images of mirrored halls and "white gloved and glittering bellied elder[s] puffed sideways at the camera" and goes on to all but dissolve music, warfare, and all in the language of sexuality—Her Vertical Smile indifferently female genitalia or Endymion's or Alastor's waning (or wax-ing?) crescent moon.

It is feasible to see these insistently *constructed* realities as manifestations of Kinsella's participation in a modernist tendency to insist on the separateness of the work of art from its putative referent, to insist on the *madeness* of art.[1] But I think that Kinsella has a more unitary sense of both reality and his art than such a concept seems to allow for, and I think moreover that his work flows more and more certainly from a model of mind at work. To come at the question from a different angle, one might acknowledge the possibility that a poem like "Butcher's Dozen" is simply dead wrong, and unjust to Widgery and paratroopers alike—that the poem is "vulnerable to history," as one commentator has put it.[2] But right or wrong, the poem is part of a mind's coming to "know" a world precisely *by* arriving at a construct, and this is the process at work in both *Her Vertical Smile* and *St. Catherine's Clock*. Seamus Deane is certainly right when he says that Kinsella's later work forms around a "dialectical relationship . . . between modes and moments of order, modes and moments of dissolution" (Deane 1985, 142). A similar dialetic between self and scene has been the subject of much of the discourse in this book, but what these later Peppercanister collections bring more vividly to light, I think, is the dialectic between *art* and scene (*scene*, of course, may include the poet-speaker's own life and nature). Kinsella's interweaving of history, personal memories, painting, music, and writing highlights a sense of the creation of a reality, a reality validated by the reasonableness and the emotional or spiritual power of the confluence of the very materials from which the poetic mind assembles it. And the reality is not flawed because it is "manufactured." For Kinsella as for Ezra Pound (and for Ludwig Wittgenstein, as it happens), that is simply the nature of realities.

It may be flawed because of other considerations, however. I have spoken earlier about the poet as predator, as Deane speaks of Kinsella's deploying "an invincible energy which marauds to create" (Deane 1985, 144). The ethical heartlessness that this can involve is written with breath-taking candor in "The Little Children" in *Songs of the Psyche*. The speaker describes playing with his infant daughter:

---

1. W. J. McCormack in fact does this in a qualified way (McCormack 1987, 71, 75).
2. Eamon Grennan, in conversation.

> I held her propped
> > by the tip of a blunt love finger
> against the kitchen wall
> > and let her topple forward
>
> one, two, three!
> > in laughter and panic
> into darkness and fire.
> > > > > (BF, 34)

The darkness and fire are figurative, but the incident is juxtaposed with the speaker's ruminations about the construction of art, and the poem ends with a grim acknowledgment of what seems to be an inevitable, brute necessity canceling utterly the human warmth of the image with which the poem began:

> At the first trace
> > of backward pressure
> the child grows unusable.

But the dialectic of poetry is not always so dark, and it *is* a dialectic, not by nature an act of predation. The aggressive ambiguity in *Her Vertical Smile*, for example, is not an imposition of language:

> Overtures and alliances.
> > White gloves advance,
> decorated bellies retire
>
> down mirrored halls.
> > Entente. Volte face.
> And seize your partner.
> And it's off to the muttonchop slaughter.
> > Belted and buttoned brilliant hosts
> march to their places line abreast.
> > > > > (VS, 11)

It is by no trick of mere poetry that these phrases fuse disparate referents. *Muttonchop slaughter* rings in a style of beard fashionable among the class that sent other men to die like mutton in slaughters like Waterloo and Verdun, and it is no trick of the poem's that the cynical treaty of Versailles was signed in a hall that seems the apotheosis of a thousand aristocratic or *haut bourgeois* ballrooms.

Nonetheless, the assertion or the construction of such all-encompassing acts of conception has to be responsibly carried out, and the ultimate locus of responsibility for a poet—perhaps for everyone—will be language, and that forms the focus of Peppercanister 14, *Personal Places*. Martin Dodsworth invoked the name of Samuel Beckett in his review of some of Kinsella's late work, referring the resemblance primarily to Kinsella's "way of seeing" and "his Swiftian horrors" (Dodsworth 1973). In the poems of *Personal Places*, some sort of relation with Beckett is indeed manifested, primarily in the weight Kinsella gives there to language and language-like behaviors. From its opening prayer, "In the name of the Father," to its closing poem on the eighteenth-century Irish poet Aogán O Rathaille, the book turns on a variety of kinds of communicative behavior—speech, kisses, tears, writing.

The short poem "After the Service" twice refers to the gestures of a principal mourner, calling into question (as in "Office for the Dead" in *Nightwalker*, over twenty years earlier) their sincerity or meaningfulness (*sc.*, responsibility):

> He stooped forward a little
> with hands held down before him
> still joined in the gesture of prayer,
> . . . .
> He stepped into the exit coach outside,
> with quick inviting hand gestures
> repeated without meaning
> and a motiveless urging in the uplifted voice.
>
> (*PP*, 13)

The very restraint here makes the poem a far more scathing commentary on received religious gestures than the more crudely outspoken "Office for the Dead" ("The grief-chewers enter . . ."—but notice also how the realism of the later poem acknowledges the plain humanity of the man, unlike the reductive attitudinizing of a phrase like "grief-chewers." The poet here does not prescribe responsibility only for others). Again and again this brief gathering of poems weighs the degree and kind of human investment that places expressive behavior more and less truly in touch with a world, from the expressive pathos of "Apostle of Hope" to the hand-to-hand combat of poets in "Brothers in the Craft":

Again and again, in the Fifties, "we" attended
Austin Clarke. He murmured in mild malice
and directed his knife-glance curiously amongst us.

Out in the dark, on a tree branch near the Bridge,
the animus of Yeats perched.
                    Another party of the City,
Tonio Kröger, malodorous, prowled Inchicore.
                                            (*PP,* 26)

On the facing page, the perfect response to such goings-on and the perfect
capstone, I believe, to what I have been arguing with respect to Kinsella's
career, "At the Western Ocean's Edge" contrasts Yeats's romanticized man
of action, Cuchulainn, whom he "found helpful as a second shadow / in
his own sour duel with the middle classes" with the figure of Aogán O
Rathaille: a language-user, doubtless defeated and in a pragmatic view
futile, but an ethical and psychic reality honored by Kinsella's poem at the
same time as his remembered existence furnishes to Thomas Kinsella the
material for the poem that honors him. Kinsella underscores his alliance
with the impoverished upright practitioner by using his own catch-phrases
from years earlier—the phrases I have italicized in these lines:

            A vagrant, turning
      the gale wailing inland off the water
      into a voice responding in his head,
      and answering the waves on their own terms
      —energy of chaos and a shaping

      counter-energy in throes of balance;
      solitary response, *eliciting*
      order from the uproar of particulars,
      struggling toward a posture of refusal
      on the basis of some kind of understanding,
      Man's beggar rags in tatters in the tempest.

No Yeatsian romanticizer, Kinsella admits:

      A wasted figure. Any substance left
      borne on waves of threat inside the mind.
      As who will not confirm, that set his face
      beyond the ninth shadow into dead calm.
      Dame Kindness, her bowels torn.
      The Stranger waiting on the steel horizon.
                                            (*PP,* 27)

A Beckettian enough vision, no doubt. But also reminiscent of Diderot, who spoke despair but conducted work. More important than a resemblance to Beckett grounded in grimness of vision is the resemblance grounded in the job assigned here to language. In much of the later Beckett there is nothing but language—the short plays *Come and Go* and *What Where* both deal, for example, with some very real horrors of modern life, horrors that are never clearly seen as action. In the latter play, the phrase "give him the works" rolls from the lips of an apparently mad dictator, directing the senseless torture of three men in succession, triggered each time by the report that "he" did not "say it":

> *Bam:* Well?
> *Bem:* [Head bowed throughout] Nothing.
> *Bam:* He didn't say where?
> *Bem:* No.
> *Voice:* So on.
> *Bam:* It's a lie. [Pause.] He said where to you. [Pause.] Confess he said where to you. [Pause.] You'll be given the works until you confess.
> *Bem:* What must I confess?
> *Bam:* That he said where to you.
>
> (Beckett 1984, 316)

The entire exchange, and Bam's exchanges with the other two characters as well, turn on words only, yet if Bam's words produce no torture actually seen, they eliminate from the stage one character after another as effectively as the Central American death squads that are Bam's probable referents remove from the public scene troublesome peasants. The words of the play are the verbal skeleton of twenty years' politico-military horrors, horrors that can be readily unleashed by a stupid B-movie phrase like "Give him the works."

The pertinence of all this to Kinsella's late work lies in the concept of the sometimes deadly sufficiency of language—in Kinsella's case the concept of a saving potentiality that is the obverse, it may be, of the nightmare aspect exploited by Beckett. An untitled poem, grimly Beckettian enough, precedes the two poems about poets that close *Personal Places:*

> There are established personal places
> that receive our time's heat
> and adapt in their mass, like stone.
>
> These absorb in their changes
> the radiance of change in us
> and give it back

to the darkness of our understanding
directionless
into the returning cold.

(PP, 25)

It would be hard to find a piece of language more sinewy than this poem, which is simultaneously circular and linear. It resembles Yeats's "After Long Silence" in taking away with one stanza what it grants in another—and in its heroic resting in the otherwise daunting, impersonal, inevitable equilibrium that is left.[3] The interanimation of self and surroundings delineated in the first two stanzas yields to the awareness of death and obliteration in the third, but the value of that joint empowerment of mind and world is no more canceled by the "returning cold" than the prospect of death is sentimentally softened by the initial interchange of warmth. The radiance of change answers to, and is answered by, the darkness of our understanding, and if what is finally presented is a relentless course of entropy, the poet's response comes in what is said about the figure of O Rathaille in "At the Western Ocean's Edge." The first two stanzas of the untitled poem delineate not the invention of a consolatory illusion in the face of mutability, but the intercreativity of the human self and its experienced reality, each validating the other, the process finding a level of authentication in the poem's fixing it in adequate language. In a way, O Rathaille in "At the Western Ocean's Edge" invokes that stance of grim stoicism that marked Kinsella's earliest work. But the transforming act of mind separates this poetry, however stoic, from that early writing. Like Jacob and the angel, the poet has wrestled with the real in the arena of language, and to speak of defeat is beside the point. To write is to "turn . . . the gale wailing inland off the water" into "a voice responding in [one's] head / and answering the waves on their own terms / —energy of chaos and a shaping / counter-energy in throes of balance." The shapeless "wail" of wind becomes a *voice* at the hands of the language-using poet. Poets, like all of us, will die; but the true poet has found—or built—that which will suffice.

Whatever Thomas Kinsella proceeds to in the years ahead, these last three collections, building on the discoveries and experiences of the work that culminates in *Peppercanister Poems 1972–1978*, clearly attain to that

3. Compare:

> Bodily decrepitude is wisdom; young
> We loved each other and were ignorant.
> (Yeats 1983, 265)

"totality" desiderated by Jung. Acknowledging with perfect realism the force of mutability and man's ultimate helplessness before it, this poetry strikes a saving blow for human dignity. It will rest content with no partial views, no incomplete lyric isolations of pleasant moments, no localist romanticisms or yearnings. That the world, the whole world, is inevadably *there,* bearing on our best and our worst moments, is a fact from which this poetry will not flinch.

Works Cited
Index

Works Cited

Arbois de Joubainville, Marie Henri d'. 1903. *The Irish Mythological Cycle and Celtic Mythology*, translated by Richard I. Best. Dublin: Hodges, Figgis.

Beckett, Samuel. 1984. *The Collected Shorter Plays*. New York: Grove Press.

Binchy, D. A. 1970. *Celtic and Anglo-Saxon Kingship*. O'Donnell Lectures for 1967–68. Oxford: Oxford Univ. Press.

Brown, Terence. 1985. *Ireland: A Social and Cultural History, 1922 to the Present*. Ithaca: Cornell Univ. Press.

Cixous, Helene. 1981. "The Laugh of the Medusa." In *New French Feminism*, edited by E. Marks and I. Courtivron. New York: Schocken.

Clarke, Austin. 1956. Review of *Poems* in *Icarus* 6, no. 20 (Nov.): 21–22.

Coogan, T. P. 1966. Ireland since the Uprising. London: Pall Mall Press.

Davie, Donald. 1957. "Review of *Poems*." *Irish Writing* 37 (Autumn): 47–49.

———. 1986. *Czeslaw Milosz and the Insufficiency of Lyric*. Knoxville: Univ. of Tennessee Press.

Dawe, Gerald. 1987. "In the Violent Zone: Thomas Kinsella's *Nightwalker and Other Poems*." *Tracks* 7:26–31.

Deane, Seamus. 1985. *Irish Revivals: Essays in Modern Irish Literature, 1880–1980*. London: Faber and Faber.

Defence and Educational Fund. 1973. *Justice Denied: A Challenge to Lord Widgery's Report on "Bloody Sunday."* New York: Defence and Educational Fund.

Dodsworth, Martin. 1968. "Review of *Nightwalker*." *The Listener*, 28 Nov.: 728.

———. 1973. "Poetry Moves to Ireland." *The Listener*, 20 Dec.: 859.

Donoghue, Denis. 1957. "Irish Writing." *The Month* n.s. 17, no. 3 (Mar.): 185.

Flower, Robin. 1947. *The Irish Tradition*. London: Oxford Univ. Press.

Gallagher, S. F. 1983. *Women in Irish Legend, Life, and Literature*. Totowa, N.J.: Barnes and Noble.

Garratt, Robert. 1986. *Modern Irish Poetry: Tradition and Continuity from Yeats to Heaney*. Berkeley: Univ. of California Press.

Haffenden, John. 1981. *Viewpoints: Poets in Conversation with John Haffenden*. London: Faber and Faber.

Hamilton, Edith, and Huntington Cairns. *The Collected Dialogues of Plato.* Bollingen Series 71. Princeton: Princeton Univ. Press.

Heaney, Seamus. 1980. *Preoccupations: Selected Prose 1968–1978.* New York: Farrar, Straus, and Giroux.

Hutchinson, Pearse. 1955. Review of *Longes Mac n-Usnech. Irish Writing* 32 (Autumn): 57–59.

Hyde, Douglas. 1906. *A Literary History of Ireland from the Earliest Times to the Present Day.* London: T. Fisher Unwin.

Jackson, Thomas H. 1968. *The Early Poetry of Ezra Pound.* Cambridge, Mass.: Harvard Univ. Press.

Jacobi, Jolande. 1951. *The Psychology of C. G. Jung,* translated by K. W. Bash. Rev. ed. New Haven: Yale Univ. Press.

Johnston, Dillon. 1985. *Irish Poetry after Joyce.* Notre Dame, Ind.: Univ. of Notre Dame Press.

Jordan, John. 1962. Off the Barricade: A Note on Three Irish Poets." In *The Dolmen Miscellany of Irish Writing.* Dublin: Dolmen Press: 107–16.

Jung, C. G. 1961. *Memories, Dreams, Reflections.* Recorded and edited by Aniela Jaffé and translated by Richard Winston and Clara Winston. New York: Pantheon.

———. 1966. *Two Essays in Analytical Psychology.* Vol. 7 of *Collected Works of C. G. Jung,* translated by R. F. C. Hull. Bollingen Series 20. Princeton: Princeton Univ. Press.

———. 1969. *Psychology and Religion: West and East.* Vol. 11 of *The Collected Works of C. G. Jung,* translated by R. F. C. Hull. Bollingen Series 20. Princeton: Princeton Univ. Press.

Kee, Robert. 1972. *The Green Flag.* 3 vols. London: Weidenfeld and Nicholson.

Kenner, Hugh. 1979. "Thomas Kinsella: An Anecdote and Some Reflection." *Genre* 12 (Winter): 591–99.

———. 1983. *A Colder Eye: The Modern Irish Writers.* New York: Alfred A. Knopf.

———. 1988. *A Sinking Island: the Modern English Writers.* New York: Alfred A. Knopf.

Kinsella, Thomas. 1958. Statement. *Poetry Society Bulletin,* no. 7 (Mar.).

———. 1962a. *Another September.* Dublin: Dolmen Press.

———. 1962b. *Downstream.* Dublin: Dolmen Press; London: Oxford Univ. Press.

———. 1967. Statement. *Poetry Society Bulletin,* no. 55 (Dec.).

———. 1968. *Nightwalker and Other Poems.* New York: Alfred A. Knopf.

———. 1969. *The Táin.* Translated by Thomas Kinsella. Oxford and Dublin: Oxford Univ. Press with Dolmen Press.

———. 1970. "The Irish Writer." In *Davis, Mangan, Ferguson? Tradition and the Irish Writer: Writings by W. B. Yeats and by Thomas Kinsella.* Edited by Roger McHugh. Dublin: Dolmen Press.

———. 1973a. "The Divided Mind." In *Irish Poets in English.* Edited by Sean Lucy, 208–18. Cork: Mercier Press.

———. 1973b. *Notes from the Land of the Dead.* New York: Alfred A. Knopf.

———. 1974. "The Poetic Career of Austin Clarke." *Irish University Review* 4, no. 1 (Spring).

———. 1976. *A Technical Supplement*. Peppercanister 6. Dublin: Peppercanister.

———. 1979a. *Peppercanister Poems 1972–1978*. Winston-Salem, N.C.: Wake Forest Univ. Press.

———. 1979b. *Poems 1956–1973*. Winston-Salem, N.C.: Wake Forest Univ. Press.

———. 1985. *Her Vertical Smile*. Dublin: Dolmen Press.

———. 1986. *The New Oxford Book of Irish Verse*. Edited by Thomas Kinsella. Oxford: Oxford Univ. Press.

———. 1988. *Blood and Family*. Oxford: Oxford Univ. Press.

———. 1990a. *Personal Places*. Dublin: Dedalus Press.

———. 1990b. *Songs of the Psyche*. Dublin: Peppercanister.

Knott, Eleanor, and Gerard Murphy. 1966. *Early Irish Literature*. London: Routledge and Kegan Paul.

Levi, Peter. 1960. Review of *Moralities*. *Civil Service Review* 17, no. 22 (July): 269.

Liddy, James. 1962. Review of *Downstream, Another September,* and *Poems and Translations*. *Kilkenny Magazine*. (Autumn-Winter): 45–48.

Lyons, F. S. L. 1973. *Ireland since the Famine*. London: Fontana Press.

Macalister, R. S. A., ed. and trans. 1938. *Lebor Gabála Erenn*, part I. Irish Texts Society 34. Dublin: Educational Company of Ireland.

———. 1956. *Lebor Gabála Erenn*, part 5. Irish Texts Society 44. Dublin: Educational Company of Ireland.

McCana, Proinsias. 1970. *Celtic Mythology*. London: Hamlyn House.

McCormack, W. J. 1987. "Politics or Community: Crux of Thomas Kinsella's Aesthetic Development." *Tracks* 7: 61–77.

Mills, Ralph. 1969. Review of *Nightwalker*. *Poetry* (Jan.): 273.

Morley, John (John Viscount Morley). 1923. *Diderot and the Encyclopædists*. 2 vols. London: Macmillan.

O'Hara, Daniel. 1981. "An Interview with Thomas Kinsella." *Contemporary Poetry: A Journal of Criticism*, 4, no. 1: 1–18.

———. 1983. "Appropriate Performance: Thomas Kinsella and the Ordeal of Understanding." In *Contemporary Irish Writing*, edited by James D. Brophy and Raymond J. Porter. Boston: Iona College Press/Twayne.

Orr, Peter. 1966. *The Poet Speaks: Interviews with Contemporary Poets*. London: Routledge and Kegan Paul.

Pound, Ezra. 1970. *Gaudier-Brzeska: A Memoir*. New York: New Directions.

Power, Patrick. 1967. *Literary History of Ireland*. Cork: Mercier Press.

Rees, Alwyn, and Brinley Rees. 1961. *Celtic Heritage*. London: Thames and Hudson.

Rosenberg, Carolyn. 1980. *Let Our Gaze Blaze: The Recent Poetry of Thomas Kinsella*. Ph.D. diss., Kent State Univ.

Rudolph, Kurt. 1983. *Gnosis: The Nature and History of Gnosticism*. Translated and edited by Robert McLachlan Wilson. San Francisco: Harper and Row.

Sharkey, John. 1975. *Celtic Mysteries*. New York: Crossroad.

Skelton, Robin. 1965. "Irish Literature and the Private Press Tradition: Dun Emer, Cuala, and Dolmen Press 1902–63." In *Irish Renaissance: A Gathering of Essays, Memoirs, and Letters for the Massachusetts Review,* edited by Robin Skelton and David R. Clarke, 158–67. Amherst: Univ. of Massachusetts Review.

Williams, William Carlos. 1988. *Collected Poems,* edited by A. Walton Litz and Christopher MacGowan. New York: New Directions.

Yeats, William Butler. 1983. *The Poems of W. B. Yeats,* edited by Richard J. Finneran. New York: Macmillan.

Index

161